Electrical 1 - DC Theory

Weekly Laboratory Manual and Rubric

2ⁿᵈ Edition

LOUIS JRAIGE

Independently Published

Louis Jraige

This weekly laboratory manual and rubric accompanies and follows the progression of the DC Electricity courses at Fanshawe College. This book also accompanies and follows the progression of the textbook titled "Introductory Circuit Analysis", 13th edition by Robert L. Boylestad and published by Pearson publishing which is used in my Electrical 1 - DC Theory course. This manual lays out the standards, expectations, conventions and best practices pertaining to scientific experimentation, data collection and analysis. Finally, this manual details the requirements for each of the weekly labs the students are expected to perform for the course including all pre-lab, experimental and post-lab work.

Program Name: _____

Course Code and Section: _____

Lab Instructor Name: _____

Student Name: _____

© 2016

Louis Jraige

I'd like to thank the graduating Electrical Engineering Technology, class of 2016, for their assistance and support. I'd also like to thank Dr. David Machacek and Fanshawe College for supporting this personal endeavor. A special thank you goes out to my mentor and friend Mr. Marko Jovanovic for his leadership, inspiration, support and impact on my life. I would like to thank my parents for their support during my transition into academia. Finally, I'd like to thank my wife Cindy and my 4 children for their inspiration, support and patience over the hundreds and hundreds of hours put in to the creation of this manual – Thank You!

A portion of the proceeds from the sale of this issue of the manual will be donated in the form of bursaries or awards setup for the hardworking students of the Electrical Engineering programs at Fanshawe College by the professor and author, Louis Jraige.

Name: _____   Date: _____   Course and Section: _____

	Proof of Absence			Grade				Validation		Notes or Comments
	Make-Up	Yes	No	Preparation	Experiment	Analysis	Extension	Signature	Date	
Lab 1										Introduction to the Lab, Safety, and Rubric
Lab 2										Introduction to the Breadboard
Lab 3										Introduction to the DMM and DC Power Supply
Lab 4										Fixed and Variable Resistors and Their Codes
Lab 5										Introduction to Multi-Sim
Lab 6										DC Series Circuits OL, JL, and KVL
Lab 7										DC Parallel Circuits OL, JL and KCL
Lab 8										DC Combination Circuits OL, JL, KVL and KCL
Lab 9										DC Superposition Theorem and Mesh Loops
Lab 10										Thevenin's and Maximum Power Transfer
Lab 11										Transient Response of Capacitors in a DC Circuit
Lab 12										Transient Response of Inductors in a DC Circuit

Fill in your name, ID number and section in permanent ink. This lab rubric is to be filled out by the instructor, facilitator or lab technician only and in permanent ink.

Please Note: Individuals who were absent during their original lab session can make it up at a later date (during an Open Lab). An Open Lab is a date set out by the instructor, facilitator or lab technician for when a student can make up or complete labs and is posted on FOL. A maximum lab grade of 10 may be earned on made up labs with valid proof that the absence was necessary and unavoidable (assessed on an individual basis and as acceptable to the instructor). Without valid proof (documentation) that the absence was necessary and unavoidable, a maximum lab grade of 1 may be earned on the lab ($P = O/E = 1/AC = 0$). For those who have come prepared, worked on the lab properly, quietly and diligently (as the exercise was intended) and for the full duration of the period but were unable to complete the Experimentation and Analysis/Conclusion. This grade (of 0 for the Experimentation and Analysis/Conclusion due to lab incompletion) may be upgraded (without penalty) in an Open Lab. For those who have come prepared, worked on the lab properly, quietly and diligently (as the exercise was intended) and for the full duration of the period but were only able to take all the required measurements/collect all the required data, an extension may be given (at the discretion of the instructor, facilitator or lab technician). If an extension is given, the Analysis and Conclusion portions of the lab will be graded the following week. If the lab is not completed and ready for grading upon the next lab session attended, a non-upgradeable grade of 0 will be recorded for the Analysis/Conclusion portion of the lab and the lab will be considered incomplete until Analysis/Conclusion portion has been completed. A lab is only considered "complete" when the signature of the instructor, facilitator or lab technician appears in the "Validation" column for that lab. It is the student's responsibility to bring this rubric to every lab, have it completed, signed by the instructor, facilitator or lab technician and submit it for permanent grade recording when required and at the end of the semester.

Mr. L. Jraige, Fanshawe College, (c) 2016

Lab Mark Rubric and Grading Structure

	3	2	1	0
This column reflects what would be considered professional conduct during the labs. This column also lists the requirements for each lab.	This column meets *all* standard criteria and indicates *"very professional"* conduct while performing labs. All must be true to fall in this category and receive this grade.	This column meets *most* standard criteria and *may still* be considered professional conduct. Any could be true to fall in this category and receive this grade.	This column meets *minimum* standard criteria and is *not* considered professional conduct. Any could be true to fall in this category and receive this score.	This column is *below standard* criteria and is *totally unprofessional and unacceptable behaviour*. Any could be true for this grade.
Preparation - 30%				
- Basic material (calculator, pencils, erasers, pencil crayons, ruler, protractor, etc.) - Tools required for the lab (wire cutters, strippers, fully functional DMM with leads, scope leads, alligator clips, PPE, etc.) - Components required for the lab (resistors, capacitors, inductors, jumpers, etc.) - Hardcopy of lab/lab manual and the grading rubric - Complete pre-lab calculations, data and/or work	- Meets all criteria (listed in the Preparation column) - Came on time and ready to start	- 1 item (listed in the Preparation column) missing - Late 0<X<=5 min	- 2 items (listed in the Preparation column) missing - Late 5<X<=15 min	- 3 or more items (listed in the Preparation column) missing - Late X>15 min - Totally un-prepared - Absent

Please Note: There may be times when certain labs have a heavy (or heavier than usual) content of pre-lab calculations or preparation. In these cases, a greater portion of the "Preparation" grade (up to the full 3 points as outlined on this rubric) may/will be allocated for that preparation. If the pre-lab requirement weight differs from what is outlined on this rubric, the new pre-lab or lab preparation weight will be indicated in the lab.

	3	2	1	0
Experimentation - 30%				
- Design circuit (if required) - Build circuit - Troubleshoot circuit - Collect all data - Demonstrate correct circuit function - Respected and followed all lab rules, procedures and standards including the use of PPE, food/drinks, conduct, etc.	- Meets all criteria (listed in the Experimentation column) - Lab is complete and data is correct - No (significant) assistance - Did not have to remind them to work quietly, wear PPE, not wonder around, etc. - Cleaned work area and put everything where they belong	- Lab is complete and data is correct - Required assistance - Small errors or a few mistakes - Had to remind them to work quietly, wear PPE, not wonder around, etc. - Partially cleaned work area and/or did not put everything where they belong	- Lab is complete and data is correct (or made up without valid documentation) - Required much assistance - Big errors or many mistakes - Had to repeatedly remind them to work quietly, wear PPE, not wonder around, etc. - Did not clean work area and/or did not put everything where they belong	- Lab is incomplete (non-functional) - Lab is incorrect (non-functional) - Absent
Analysis/Conclusion - 40%	3 +1 *2	2	1	0
- Analyzed data and fully answer all related problems - Neatly, fully, and correctly completed tables and graphs - Provided a detailed conclusion	- Meets all criteria (listed in the Analysis column)	- 1 item (listed in the Analysis column) missing	- 2 items (listed in the Analysis column) missing	- 3 items (listed in the Analysis column) missing

*2 *Please Note:* The outstanding 10% in this category is an overall "professionalism" grade and is intended to grade the overall accuracy and presentation of the lab report. The 10% grade will be with held from labs that are not considered "very professional" (3's in all categories).

Class and Lab Expectation and Clarification Contract

Please read the Academic Policy 2-G-04 before signing this document. The link is provided below:

https://www.fanshawec.ca/sites/default/files/legacy/oldfanshawe/sites/default/files/assets/policies/pdf/2g04.pdf

There will be "Zero Tolerance" for cheating, copying or plagiarism of any kind. Any one (either individually or in a group) found to be in violation of Academic Policy 2-G-04 will be subject to discipline by the terms of Academic Policy 2-G-04 up to and including suspension or expulsion.

The items below are meant to clarify a few points that may be "gray".

1) All summative evaluated work is to be completed individually and with no external aids of any kind. This includes Term Tests, Lab Tests, Theory Exams, Practical Exams, etc. Those students who require accommodations to complete evaluated work may be allowed to have those aids outlined on their accommodation form with them.

2) All formative evaluated work may be completed individually with the help of external aids. This includes homework assignments, lab assignments, etc. This does not mean that if working in a group, one person does the work "with the help of others" and then everyone copies the work. Copying someone else's work or submitting someone else's work as your own violates of the spirit of the formative evaluation. When working in a group, each member will do their own work and, if stuck, may ask another group member for assistance or clarification.

3) Please come to labs and class on time. It is very distracting to come into class or labs late. In the case of labs, and in accordance with the Lab Rubric, there are grade penalties that will be applied for late entries to the lab. If you are found coming in late to the lab or class on a regular basis, you will no longer be allowed entry after the top of the hour.

4) In my course, safety is paramount! We will respect all rules designed to keep people, furniture, equipment and property safe! PPE must be worn at all times while in the lab. No food will be allowed in the classrooms or lab rooms. Drinks will be allowed in "sealed" containers. A container will be considered sealed if it can be turned up-side-down and shaken violently with no liquid leaving the container. Otherwise, you will be asked to leave your drink at the front of the room where you are welcome to drink from it during your lab or to get it at the end of class.

5) It is the responsibility of the student to ensure they come to class and labs prepared. This means when coming to class, the student must have their textbook, solution manual, completed homework assignments, writing utensils and calculator with them. When coming to the lab, it is the students responsibility to have with them their lab manual, completed pre-lab, program kit (including PPE and DMM), course lab kit, all the components required to complete the lab, writing utensils and calculator with them. Although it is the student's responsibility to come to the lab prepared, in the event a student is missing a component, PPE or DMM, the Lab Technician may try and accommodate by lending the missing item to a student for the duration of the lab session.

Louis Jraige

6) Remember, placing book bags or tool bags on the desktops is strictly prohibited as things like this are the biggest culprits to equipment damage.

7) Attendance to the lab and lecture must occur during the dates and times outlined on the schedule assigned by the registrar's office. The only acceptation is in the event of a missed lab that may be made up during an "Open Lab" (in accordance with the Lab Rubric and the course CIS.

      I _____ will treat the classroom and lab room furniture and equipment with respect as long as I am a student in the _____ program. Should I find any damaged property or if I accidentally damage property, I will report it to my professor or lab instructor immediately. I will also come to my classes and labs prepared to the best of my ability. This includes completing all my homework assignments and all of my lab preparation as outlined on my lab rubric.

      I have read and fully understood what is expected of me both in class and in the lab. I have received clarification on anything I wasn't sure of and fully agree with what was listed. Finally, I have read got clarification and fully understood Academic Policy 2-G-04.

_____   _____
     Professors Name   Lab Technician's Name

_____   _____   _____
Print Name   Signature   Date

Bill of Materials

The following is a bill (or list) of material required to complete all the labs presented in this manual:

Required College Supplied Material

- Circuit-Test   PS-3330   Single Fixed/Dual Variable DC Power Supply
- Topward   8110   Function Generator
- Tektronix   TDS1001B   Two Channel Digital Storage Oscilloscope

- Resistors: Set of Ten Assorted Resistor Values *(1 - Supplied by Fanshawe College)*
- Potentiometers: Single Potentiometer of Unknown Value *(1 - Supplied by Fanshawe College)*
- Decade Resistance box *(1 - Supplied by Fanshawe College)*

Required Material Supplied in your Program Kit

- Your PPE (untinted/untreated, CSA approved safety glasses with side shields)
- Your tool and component kits (see your CIS on FOL)
- A breadboard, jumper wires and alligator leads
- Wire cutters and strippers (if you don't plan on using the premade jumpers)
- Your DMM (Digital Multi-Meter – MTP 2327)
- Your calculator (Sharp EL-516)
- Various coloured pencil crayons (at least 12 different colours)
- A math set (at least a ruler and protractor)

Required Material Supplied in your Course Kit

- Power Resistors: 100 Ω (5 Watt Power Resistor)
- Potentiometers: *1 kΩ (1), 10 kΩ (1), 100 kΩ (1)*
- Trim Potentiometers: *10 kΩ (1),*
- Capacitors: *4.7 nF (1), 47 nF (1), 0.1 µF (1), 1 µF (1), 10 µF (1),* 100 µF (1)
- Inductors: *1 mH (1), 10 mH (1),* 100 mH (1)
- Batteries: *9 Volt Battery (1)*
- Fuses: *250 mA glass protection fuse for the DMM (10)*

Required Material Supplied in your Lab Kit

- Complete and Sorted Resistor Kit (including the following resistors):
- 100 Ω (1), 330 Ω (1), 470 Ω (1),
- 1 kΩ (1), 1.2 kΩ (1), 1.5 kΩ (1), 2 kΩ (1), 2.2 kΩ (1), 2.7 kΩ (1), 3.3 kΩ (1), 4.7 kΩ (2), 5.6 kΩ (1), 6.8 k Ω (1), 10 kΩ (1), 100 kΩ (1) and 1 MΩ (1)

Required Material NOT Supplied

- A stopwatch *(or a timer that can measure seconds – most people use a mobile app for this)*

Optional Material You May Want to Purchase

- A pair of tweezers
- A magnifying glass (with or without light)
- A flashlight
- A small Phillips screw driver
- A small flat screwdriver

Required Consumable Material *(Material You Should Expect to Replace)*

- 250 mA glass protection fuse for the "current measurement circuit" of the DMM
- 9 Volt battery for the DMM

Louis Jraige

Table of Contents

Louis Jraige

Louis Jraige

Introduction to the Lab, Lab Safety, the Rubric, Standards and Expectations

Name: _____   Course and Section: _____

Partner: _____   Date: _____

PURPOSE:

The purpose of this lab is to become familiar with the following:
1. Electrical safety and how to safely conduct ourselves while in the lab.
2. Get clarification on what is expected as far as PPE, food and drinks in the lab, etc.
3. Become familiar with industry wiring standards, neatness expectation, etc.
4. Understand the lab grading structure and how to read and use the rubric.

EQUIPMENT:

1. Your tool and component kits (see your CIS on FOL)
2. Your PPE (untinted/untreated, CSA approved safety glasses with side shields)
3. Electrical safety video (Supplied by Fanshawe College)
4. A blue pen and a black marker or Sharpie.

PREPARATION:

Please read and fill out the "Class and Lab Expectation and Clarification Contract" found in introductory portion of this manual before coming in to the lab. Do not sign and date it yet as this will be done as a group in the lab and only after a group discussion on safety.

Louis Jraige

DESIGN INTENT:

Please refer to the lab purpose.

BACKGROUND DATA:

TEXTBOOK REFERENCE:

PROCEDURE:

Because this is our first lab, we will only engage in discussion and observe in-lab demonstrations. However, beginning next week, you will be required to have your course kit, lab kit and DMM purchased from the book store.

The following are notes to the Lab Instructor:

Please fill in the program name, lab instructors name, the course code and your name on the appropriate page in the introductory portion of this manual.

Also, please review the "Lab Marking Rubric and Grading Structure". Have the students fill out their name, the date, the course and section after the discussion.

Next, please review the "Class and Lab Expectation and Clarification Contract". Have the students fill out their name, program name and section in the body of the contract and the professor's name, the lab instructors name, their name, the date and signature at the bottom. Please collect the contracts after the discussion and signing.

Finally, go around and have the students write their name, course code and section along the top edge of the lab manual pages. This will deter theft, help keep your manual safe and prevent someone from taking credit for your work.

After all the paperwork has been done and collected, please watch the safety video and discuss the specific safety requirements for our labs. Also, share stories about electrical safety with the students and have them share some of their experiences with everyone.

Louis Jraige

ANALYSIS/OBSERVATIONS:

1) What the lab policy is on wearing your safety glasses?

2) When is an acceptable time to not be wearing your safety glasses?

3) When are the accepted times to put them on and take them off?

4) Where must your backpacks and tool boxes reside while in the lab?

5) Where must they never be while in the lab?

6) If you run into a problem while working on your circuits, what are the steps you **must** follow to resolve your problem? Please state them in the order they are to be performed.

7) Why must we follow the above steps? What advantage do they offer in regards to learning to troubleshooting properly?

8) If you run into a problem while working on your circuits, what must you never do and why?

9) Do you have to complete every lab?

10) If you have missed a lab, how must it be made up?

11) What is the advantage of completing the pre-lab? What would be the maximum grade earned on a lab if you came to the lab without your pre-lab complete, missing some components (like your resistors or DMM) and without your rubric and why?

CONCLUSION:

In the space provided below, please write down what is expected in a "complete" and proper conclusion.

Since this is our first week of class, everyone <u>present</u> will earn full marks for this lab. If missed (unless special permission is given), the <u>only</u> marks available will be for the Analysis and Conclusion.

Louis Jraige

Introduction to the Breadboard, Engineering Notation and Your Calculator (Sharp EL-516)

Name: _____   Course and Section: _____

Partner: _____   Date: _____

PURPOSE:

The purpose of this lab is to become familiar with the following:
1. How to use a Breadboard (or prototype boards).
2. Powers of 10 and Engineering Notation.
3. Using your calculator's Engineering Notation functionality.

EQUIPMENT:

1. Your tool and component kits (see your CIS on FOL)
2. Your PPE (untinted/untreated, CSA approved safety glasses with side shields)
3. A breadboard, jumper wires and alligator leads
4. Your DMM (Digital Multi-Meter – MTP 2327)
5. Your calculator (Sharp EL-516)
6. Battery: 9 Volt (1)

PREPARATION:

1) Please read the document labeled "Breadboard Connections" (Appendix A) and the section of the "The DMM" (Appendix B) that deals with locating and replacing the battery prior to completing the pre-lab.

2) Next, please watch the YouTube video located at the following link. The link below is posted on our FOL course homepage in the news announcement for this lab week. Accessing it from FOL might be easier than typing it in. https://www.youtube.com/watch?v=q_Q5s9AhCR0

3) Please install the 9 Volt battery that came with your kit (not the battery that comes with your DMM) into the DMM. The battery that comes with your DMM is just a starter battery and does not contain much of a charge.

4) *Finally, please sketch in pencil the connection points of* **ALL** *the sockets shown on the image below.*

© 2016

Louis Jraige

DESIGN INTENT:

     In this lab we will be investigating the proper use of a breadboard. We will also learn how to properly use the continuity function of a DMM to map out the internal connections of the breadboard. We will investigate the use of engineering notation both manually and with our calculator. Please read the document labeled "Breadboard Connections" (Appendix A) prior to completing the lab.

BACKGROUND DATA:

TEXTBOOK REFERENCE:

PROCEDURE:

1. **Introduction to the Breadboard**
   1.1 Take out or locate two jumper wires (any length).
   1.2 Insert your black DMM lead into the common (or reference) "COM" terminal and your red DMM lead into the active VΩHz terminal.
   1.3 Your DMM has a function called continuity   ))   or   ♫   which is used to test whether 2 points are connected. Set the DMM selector switch to its continuity setting and then turn it on.
   1.4 Touch the two DMM leads together and listen for the audible tone. This tone tells you that the two leads are in electrical contact.
   1.5 Touch each of the DMM leads to the either end of the jumper wire. Document what you see on the display and hear from your meter.
   What you see on the display: _____
   What you hear: _____
   1.6 Remove only the red lead and document what you see on the display and hear from your meter.
   1.7 Reconnect the red lead, remove only the black lead and document what you see on the display and hear from your meter.
   What you see on the display: _____
   What you hear: _____
   1.8 Use your alligator leads (or a set of double-ended alligator cords) to attach 2 jumper wires to your DMM (one jumper to your black lead and one to your red lead).
   1.9 Use your DMM to verify your pre-lab diagram is correct by "beeping out" the points you think are connected and verifying the points you think are not connected.
   1.10 Make any necessary corrections to your pre-lab diagram you think might be necessary.

2. **Powers of 10 and Engineering Notation**
   2.1 Without the use of a calculator, write the following numbers in Scientific and Engineering Notation in Powers of 10 *(Example: 1.0 x 10³)*:
   NOTE: The "" indicates that the instructor will "take up in class".*

	* 10 000 Ω	* 0.3 A	500 V	649 000 000 Ω	1 234 567 890 Ω	0.00025 A
Scientific Notation						
Engineering Notation						

Table 2.2.1

2.2 Without the use of a calculator, perform the following calculations and express your final answer in Engineering Notation in Powers of 10. *(Example: 1.0 x 10³)*:

	47 000 Ω + 2 500 Ω + 30 Ω	* 0.0025 A + 0.00049 A + 0.07 A	10 V + 25 V + 36 V + 75 V
Manual Calculation (Manual Addition of the Numbers Shown)			
Write the above Answers (Sums) in Engineering Notation			

Table 2.2.2

2.3 Rewrite the above solutions from steps 2.1 and 2.2 in Engineering Notation with Prefixes. *(Example: milli, kilo, etc.)*.

2.1 Values →	10 000 Ω	0.3 A	500 V	649 000 000 Ω	* 1 234 567 890 Ω	0.00025 A
Engineering Notation with Prefixes						

Table 2.2.3

2.2 Values →			
Engineering Notation with Prefixes			

Table 2.2.4

3. Engineering Notation and Your calculator (Sharp EL-516)

3.1 To put your calculator into Engineering Mode you must first turn it on (On / C), select the (SET UP) option by pushing the second function button (2nd F), and then the button labelled math (MATH). Select the FSE option (1), then the ENG option (2) and to set the precision (number of decimals) to three decimal places, set the "Tab" option to (3).

3.2 Your calculator should now read "0.000ᴇ00".

3.3 To use your calculator in engineering notation you would first enter the mantissa (the coefficient or the product) and then the push the (Exp) button to enter the exponent. The base is understood to be 10 already. For example, to enter the number 25,300 you could type in 25.3 $\times 10^{03}$ by entering 25.3 (Exp) 03. If you wanted to enter 0.0253 you could type in 25.3 $\times 10^{-03}$ by entering 25.3 (Exp) (+/-) 03.

3.4 If your answers come out as a fraction, use the │CHANGE│ button to convert it to a decimal.

3.5 Enter the values as they appear in step 2.1 in your calculator and record your answer.

	10 000 Ω	0.3 A	500 V	649 000 000 Ω	1 234 567 890 Ω	0.00025 A
Calculator Displayed Value						

Table 2.3.1

3.6 Enter the equations as they appear in step 2.2 in your calculator and record your answer.

	47 000 Ω + 2 500 Ω + 30 Ω	0.0025 A + 0.00049 A + 0.07 A	10 V + 25 V + 36 V + 75 V
Calculator Displayed Value			

Table 2.3.2

Louis Jraige

ANALYSIS/OBSERVATIONS:

1) In the space below, please make a comparison of the format of values expressed in scientific notation verses those expressed in engineering notation.

2) What is the primary advantage of using Engineering Notation?

3) Describe the number expression standard we will be using for our course and why that standard was chosen?

4) When performing multistep calculations (with numbers calculated in previous steps), what value format will we be using in class, on evaluations and in the labs and why?

5) List 3 instances in your life you would use values expressed in Engineering Notation with prefixes.

CONCLUSION:

Please write down 3 things you learned today in the space provided below. As always with a technical report, be sure to write a detailed conclusion addressing the purpose of the lab and referencing your analysis, observations and experimentation results for support.

After your lab has been signed off and you have cleaned up your work station, please go around to see if others need help and assist (not distract) them. Remember, we assist by making observations and asking questions with our hands behind our backs.

Grade Breakdown Structure

(Refer to your Weekly Lab Rubric or the Sample Rubric posted in your lab manual for more detail.)

	Lab: The Breadboard, Engineering Notation and Calculator	Score				
1	Section 1 – Preparation		3	2	1	0
2	Section 2 – Experimentation		3	2	1	0
3	Section 3 – Analysis, Conclusion and Professionalism	4	3	2	1	0
Notes/Comments:		**Total**				
		Teacher's Signature (above)				
		Name				
		Date				

Louis Jraige

Introduction to the DMM and DC Power Supply

Name: _____   Course and Section: _____

Partner: _____   Date: _____

PURPOSE:

The purpose of this lab is to become familiar with the following:
1. Properly measure voltage and current with a DMM.
2. Properly use a power supply in both the constant voltage and constant current modes.
3. Investigate power supply loading affects.
4. Test the DMM's over current protection fuse.
5. Locate both the over current fuse and battery in a DMM.
6. Determine the accuracy of our DMM and power supply.

EQUIPMENT:

1. Your tool and component kits (see your CIS on FOL)
2. Your PPE (untinted/untreated, CSA approved safety glasses with side shields)
3. A breadboard, jumper wires and alligator leads
4. Your DMM (Digital Multi-Meter – MTP 2327)
5. A small Phillips screw driver (1)
6. 100 Ω (5 Watt Power Resistor) (1)

PREPARATION:

Please use the internet to find the resolution and accuracy of the MTP 2327 DMM and the meter accuracy of the PS-3330 power supply. Please make sure you have read the documents labeled "The DMM" (Appendix B) and "The Power Supply" (Appendix C) prior to completing the pre-lab.

Table 3.0.1

DMM - DC Voltage		
Range	Resolution	Accuracy
200 mV		
2 V		
20 V		
200 V		
1000 V		

Table 3.0.2

DMM - DC Current		
Range	Resolution	Accuracy
2 mA		
20 mA		
200 mA		
10 A		

Meter accuracy of the power supply: _____

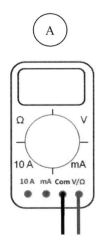

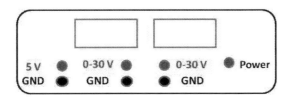

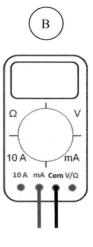

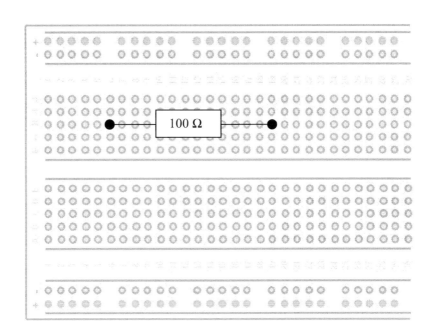

Please use the following conventions:

Red wires for (+)

Black wires for (-).

Blue wires for jumpers.

Grey ─□─ for resistors.

Black ● for node connections.

Using the appropriate coloured pencil crayons (red and black), connect the circuit so that the power supply's "Master" is applying 15 VDC across the resistor. Connect DMM A to measure the voltage across the resistor and DMM B to measure the current through the resistor. Be sure to show the power supply's meter movement position and the DMM's selector switch positions. Also, be sure to use only straight (or 90º bent) lines created with a ruler and connection nodes where appropriate for all connections. Please read the introduction of Appendix K (Our Course and Lab Standards) and the section titled "Direct Connections and Wire Crossings" in the "Schematic and Wiring Diagram Standards" section.

Louis Jraige

DESIGN INTENT:

In this lab we will be investigating the proper use of a power supply and Digital Multi-Meter (DMM). We will learn how to properly connect a power supply to a load. We will also investigate the proper use of a DMM, how to test and change its fuse and replace the battery. We will also learn how to properly take voltage and current measurements. Please make sure you have read the documents labeled "The DMM" (Appendix B) and "The Power Supply" (Appendix C) prior to completing the lab.

BACKGROUND DATA:

TEXTBOOK REFERENCE:

PROCEDURE:

1. **Using the Power Supply and Performing DMM Measurements**

   1.1 Set your DMM to measure resistance by connecting the test leads to the correct sockets on your DMM and setting the DMM's rotary selector switch to measure resistance on the 200 Ω range.

   1.2 As always, connect the resistor to your breadboard. Remember, when building any circuit, you must use a breadboard. Connect your DMM test leads across the power resistor. Record the resistor's resistance: $R_1 = $ _____ Ω

   1.3 Turn all the potentiometers (knobs) on the "Master" side of the power supply fully counter-clockwise (CCW) then turn the "Current" potentiometer clockwise (CW) one third of a turn.

   1.4 Turn the power supply on. ___*Note:*___ *This particular power supply has a built in current limiting circuit whose limit can be adjusted by the "Current" potentiometer. In the event of a short circuit or other over current condition, the power supply will attempt to limit the output current (make it constant) and any measurements you take during this time will be incorrect. You must either remove the short circuit (if there is one) or increase the current limit (until the red "CC" light shuts off and the green "CV" light turns on). Then you can resume your work.*

   1.5 Use the "coarse" potentiometer to adjust the output voltage to just under 15 VDC mark on the power supply's built-in analog voltmeter. If your power supply does not put out the correct voltage, you may have a faulty alligator lead (or jumper). You will have to test and replace it.

   1.6 Use the "fine" potentiometer to adjust (or fine tune) the output voltage to exactly the 15 VDC mark on the power supply's built-in analog voltmeter. Record the analog output voltage: $V_{Out(Analog)} = $ _____ VDC

   1.7 Turn the power supply off.

   1.8 Set your DMM to measure voltage by connecting the test leads to the correct sockets on your DMM and set the DMM's rotary selector switch to measure DC voltage on the 20 V range.

   1.9 Connect your DMM across the "Master" side power supply terminals.

   1.10 Turn the power supply on.

   1.11 Record the unloaded output voltage: $V_{Out(DMM)} = $ _____ VDC

   1.12 Reverse the DMM leads and re-measure the output voltage: $V_{Out(DMM)} = $ _____ VDC

   1.13 Turn the power supply off.

   1.14 Connect the power resistor across the power supply's "Master" side "5-way" binding posts.

   1.15 Turn the power supply on and without changing any of the potentiometers, retake the output voltage measurement with your DMM.
   Record the loaded output voltage: $V_{R(Full-Load)} = $ _____ VDC

   1.16 Use the power supply's analog ammeter and measure the current using the 0 A to 3 A scale.
   Record the resistor's load current: $I_{R(Analog)} = $ _____ mA

   1.17 Turn the power supply off.

   1.18 Set your DMM to measure current by connecting the test leads to the correct sockets on your DMM and set the DMM's rotary selector switch to measure DC current on the 200 mA range.

   1.19 Connect your DMM in series (or inline) with the power resistor by disconnecting the resistor from the power supply and inserting the DMM between them.

   1.20 Turn the power supply on and measure the load current. If you read 0.00 mA for the current, you may have blown your fuse. Please jump to Sections 2 then 3 and then come back to finish.
   Record the resistor's load current: $I_{R(DMM)} = $ _____ mA

   1.21 Reverse the DMM leads and re-measure the load current: $I_{R(DMM)} = $ _____ mA

   1.22 Turn the power supply's "Current" potentiometer counter-clockwise (CCW) until the green "CV" (constant voltage) light shuts off and the red "CC" (constant current) light turns on. Move the knob back and forth. Notice and write what has happens to the voltage and current levels. _____

2. Test the DMM's Over Current Protection Fuse

You will need the assistance of a classmate sitting next to you for this next section. Between the two of you, you will decide who will be DMM (A) and who will be DMM (B)

2.1 To test a DMM for a blown fuse (over current protection), set the suspect DMM (B) to the ammeter function and on the 200 mA range.

2.2 Set DMM (A) to its audible continuity test mode to verify that the fuse is intact (not blown).

2.3 Connect the DMM (A)'s test leads to DMM (B)'s test leads.

2.4 If you can hear the "beeping" of the piezoelectric buzzer, then the fuse is intact however, if there is no "beep" then the fuse has been blown and must be replaced.

2.5 Repeat steps 2.1 to 2.4 but this time, swap the roles of the DMMs. DMM (B) will perform the continuity test and verify the state of DMM (A)'s fuse.

3. Locating the DMM's Over Current Protection Fuse and Battery

3.1 To replace the battery, simply remove the screw holding the battery cover on. Replace the battery if required and then replace the battery cover. Be sure to insert the protrusions into the recesses before tightening the screw.

3.2 To replace the fuse, you must first remove the blue protective holster from the back of the DMM.

3.3 Next, remove the four small corner screws from the back of the DMM and remove the back cover. Do not remove the battery cover screw as it is not required. Place the cover aside. Do not tug on the battery connector wire as they are fragile and could break.

3.4 Next, use your pliers and remove the defective fuse and replace it with a new one if required. Be careful when removing the fuse from the PCB so as not to damage the board or fuse holder.

3.5 After the fuse has been replaced, return the back cover, tighten the four corner screws and replace the blue protective cover.

ANALYSIS/OBSERVATIONS:

1) What observations can you make when reviewing and comparing the data collected in steps 1.6/1.11 and 1.16/1.20? What possible sources of error can you list here?

2) What observations can you make when reviewing and comparing the data collected in steps 1.11/1.12 and 1.20/1.21? Why do you think it is so?

3) What observations can you make when reviewing and comparing the data collected in steps 1.11 and 1.15? What is this error phenomena called?

4) What observations can you make when reviewing the data collected in steps 1.22?

Louis Jraige

CONCLUSION:

Please draw a conclusion based on the purpose of this lab and referencing your observations and the lab's supporting documents.

After your lab has been signed off and you have cleaned up your work station, please go around to see if others need help and assist (not distract) them. Remember, we assist by making observations and asking questions with our hands behind our backs.

Grade Breakdown Structure

(Refer to your Weekly Lab Rubric or the Sample Rubric posted in your lab manual for more detail.)

	Lab: The DMM and DC Power Supply		Score			
1	Section 1 – Preparation		3	2	1	0
2	Section 2 – Experimentation		3	2	1	0
3	Section 3 – Analysis, Conclusion and Professionalism	4	3	2	1	0
Notes/Comments:		**Total**				
		Teacher's Signature (above)				
		Name				
		Date				

Introduction to Resistors and the Colour Code

Name: _____   Course and Section: _____

Partner: _____   Date: _____

PURPOSE:

The purpose of this lab is to become familiar with the following:
1. Use the standard colour code to determine a resistors nominal value.
2. Use your digital multi-meter (DMM) to measure a resistors actual value.
3. Determine the resistors tolerance and expected resistance range
4. Calculate the percent difference between the actual and measured resistance values.
5. Determine a potentiometer's terminal labels and measure their relative resistance.
6. To become intimately familiar with the grading expectations on labs and evaluations.

EQUIPMENT:

1. Your tool and component kits (see your CIS on FOL)
2. Your PPE (untinted/untreated, CSA approved safety glasses with side shields)
3. Jumper wires and alligator leads
4. Your DMM (Digital Multi-Meter – MTP 2327)
5. Your calculator (Sharp EL-516)
6. Resistors: Set of Ten Assorted Resistor Values *(1 - Supplied by Fanshawe College)*
7. Potentiometers: 10 kΩ Trim Potentiometer (1), Single Potentiometer of Unknown Value *(1 - Supplied by Fanshawe College)*

PREPARATION: *For full marks, please show **all** your work (in our course standard form) when performing calculations.*

Please read the document labeled "Resistors and their Code Schemes" (Appendix D) and the sections titled "Grading Breakdown Structure" and "Problem and Solution Example" in Appendix K prior to completing the pre-lab.

1) *Determine the resistor colour code for the following Resistors:*

(a) *14 Ω @ 5%*   _____

(b) *4.7 kΩ @ 10%*   _____

(c) *820 Ω @ 20%*   _____

(d) *5.6 MΩ @ 10%*   _____

(e) *1.0 Ω @ 5%*   _____

© 2016

Louis Jraige

2) *Determine the nominal (R_{nom}) resistance values and tolerances for the following colour codes:*

(a) *orange – red – black – gold* _____

(b) *violet – yellow – brown – silver* _____

(c) *blue – green – brown – none* _____

(d) *white – orange – gold – silver* _____

(e) *grey – red – yellow – gold* _____

3) *Explain how you would use your DMM to identify the terminals of a potentiometer:*

_____

_____

_____

4) *Please determine the all the following quantities. Be sure to show every calculation (and (as always) in our standard format) for every quantity below.*

14 Ω @ 5% $\Delta R =$ _____ $R_{UL} =$ _____ $R_{LL} =$_____

4.7 kΩ @ 10% $\Delta R =$ _____ $R_{UL} =$ _____ $R_{LL} =$_____

820 Ω @ 20% $\Delta R =$ _____ $R_{UL} =$ _____ $R_{LL} =$_____

5.6 MΩ @ 10% $\Delta R =$ _____ $R_{UL} =$ _____ $R_{LL} =$ _____

1.0 Ω @ 5% $\Delta R =$ _____ $R_{UL} =$ _____ $R_{LL} =$ _____

5) *If the following values were measured for the resistors in Pre-Lab Section 4, determine the difference (as a percent) between the resistors measured value and its nominal value. Be sure to show every calculation for every quantity on the back of this page.*

15 Ω $Diff_{(\%)} =$ _____

4.5 kΩ $Diff_{(\%)} =$ _____

850 Ω $Diff_{(\%)} =$ _____

5.4 MΩ $Diff_{(\%)} =$ _____

1.0 Ω $Diff_{(\%)} =$ _____

6) *Please use the "Grading Breakdown Structure" to grade your calculation in sections 4 and 5 of this pre-lab and record your grade (out of 40) below. Then calculate your grade as a percent.*

Louis Jraige

DESIGN INTENT:

In this lab we will be investigating fixed and variable resistors. Please make sure you have read the document labeled "Resistors and Code Schemes" (Appendix D) prior to completing the lab.

BACKGROUND DATA:

TEXTBOOK REFERENCE:

PROCEDURE:

1. **Introduction to Resistors**

   1.1 Locate the set of assorted resistors and orient it so that the first resistor (#1) is on top. You will only be doing half of the resistors on the resistor strip. The instructor will assign you to complete either the even or odd numbered resistors.

   1.2 Orient the assorted resistor set so that the colour bands, if read from left to right, would have the first value band (coloured) on the left and the tolerance band (Gold, Silver or None) on the right.

   1.3 Read and record the (three, four or five) colour bands in Table 4.1.1.

   1.4 Determine and record the resistors nominal value and percent tolerance in Table 4.1.1.

   1.5 Calculate the upper and lower limits of the resistance value and record them in Table 4.1.1.

   1.6 Use your DMM (set to the correct pre-determined range) to measure the resistors actual resistance value and record it in Table 4.1.1.

   1.7 Calculate the percent difference between the measured resistance and the nominal resistance and record it in Table 4.1.1.

   1.8 Determine if the measured value was within the predetermined range.

   1.9 Repeat steps 1.2 to 1.8 for the remaining four resistors.

2. **Introduction to Potentiometers**

   2.1 Locate the trim and body mountable potentiometers.

   2.2 Read, decode and record the trim potentiometers value in Table 4.2.1.

   2.3 Identify the body mountable potentiometer's terminals. Use your DMM (set to the correct range) to measure the body mountable potentiometers terminal resistances R_{AB}, R_{BC} and R_{AC} and record them in Table 4.2.2.

   2.4 Calculate the percent difference between the measured resistance (R_{AC}) and the nominal resistance of the potentiometer and record them in Table 4.2.2.

3. **Introduction to the Grading Breakdown Structure**

   3.1 Using the "Grading Breakdown Structure", please grade your "neighbours" work for section 1 of the procedure (as indicated by "*") as if they were calculations on a test in their lab manual.

   3.2 Then calculate their final grade for those "test solutions" as a percentage (out of 40) and return their manual to them.

Louis Jraige

ANALYSIS/OBSERVATIONS:

Please use the space below to capture/record your data/information or to answer questions. For full marks, please show **_all_** your work when performing calculations.

	First Assigned Resistor	Second Assigned Resistor	Third Assigned Resistor	Fourth Assigned Resistor	Fifth Assigned Resistor
1st Band Colour					
2nd Band Colour					
3rd Band Colour					
4th Band Colour					
Nominal Value (Ω)					
* Tolerance (%)					
* Upper Limit (Ω)					
* Lower Limit (Ω)					
Measured Value (Ω)					
* Difference (%)					

Table 4.1.1

	Trim Potentiometer Value
1st Digit	
2nd Digit *(if available)*	
Power of Ten Multiplier	
Nominal Value of Pot (kΩ)	

Table 4.2.1

	Body Mounted Potentiometer		
	Fully Clockwise (CW)	Fully Counter-Clockwise (CCW)	Set to 1/3 CW
R_{AB} (kΩ)			
R_{BC} (kΩ)			
R_{AC} (kΩ)			
$R_{AB} + R_{BC}$ (kΩ)			
Difference (%) of R_{AC} & $R_{NOMINAL}$			

Table 4.2.2

Louis Jraige

CONCLUSION:

Please describe in detail which lab objectives you met (if any) and how they were achieved.

After your lab has been signed off and you have cleaned up your work station, please go around to see if others need help and assist (not distract) them. Remember, we assist by making observations and asking questions with our hands behind our backs.

Grade Breakdown Structure

(Refer to your Weekly Lab Rubric or the Sample Rubric posted in your lab manual for more detail.)

	Lab: Introduction to Resistors and the Colour Code	Score				
1	Section 1 – Preparation		3	2	1	0
2	Section 2 – Experimentation		3	2	1	0
3	Section 3 – Analysis, Conclusion and Professionalism	4	3	2	1	0
Notes/Comments:		**Total**				
		Teacher's Signature (above)				
		Name				
		Date				

Introduction to MultiSim

Name: _____   Course and Section: _____

Partner: _____   Date: _____

PURPOSE:

The purpose of this lab is to become familiar with the following:
1. Investigate Ohm's Law and Joule's Law (Power Law).
2. Introduce the student to the electrical/electronic simulation software MultiSim.
3. To become intimately familiar with the grading expectations on labs and evaluations.

EQUIPMENT:

1. Your PPE (untinted/untreated, CSA approved safety glasses with side shields)
2. Your calculator (Sharp EL-516)

PREPARATION: *For full marks, please show **all** your work (in our course standard form) when performing calculations.*

1) Determine what XMM1 (the ammeter), the XMM2 (the voltmeter) and XWM1 (the wattmeter) DMMs should read if the circuit was connected correctly and is functioning properly.

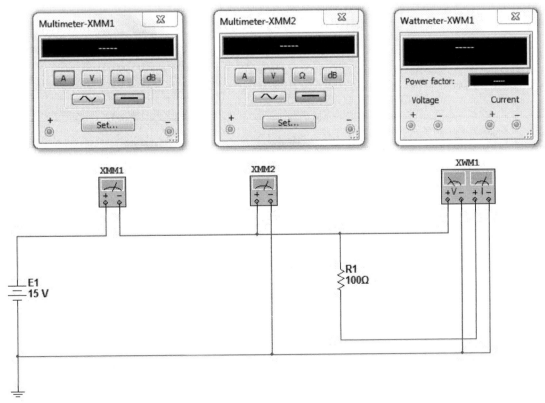

Louis Jraige

$V_{R1(XMM2)} =$

$I_{R1(XMM1)} =$

$P_{R1(XWM1)} =$

Look up the V_{R1}, I_{R1} and P_{R1} from the lab results to the experiment performed in Lab 3 (2 weeks ago - Introduction to the DMM and DC Power Supply) and record them below.

$V_{R1} =$ _____ , $I_{R1} =$ _____ , $P_{R1} =$ _____

2) *Please make sure you have read the document labeled "Introduction to Multi-Sim" (Appendix E) prior to coming to the lab.*

3) *Finally, please watch the YouTube videos located at the following links. The links below are posted on our FOL course homepage in the news announcement for this lab week. Accessing them from FOL might be easier than typing them in.*

   https://www.youtube.com/watch?v=WbSGoJsNB98

   https://www.youtube.com/watch?v=IkWpMoHXGpo

4) *Grade your pre-lab calculations based on our grading structure (out of 6) and record your final grade as a percent below.*

DESIGN INTENT:

In this lab we will be learn how to use the National Instruments software called Multi-Sim and use Multi-Sim to investigate Ohm's and Joule's Laws. Please make sure you have read the document labeled "Introduction to Multi-Sim" (Appendix E) and watch the video link located on the FOL news announcement prior to completing the lab.

BACKGROUND DATA:

TEXTBOOK REFERENCE:

Louis Jraige

PROCEDURE:

Before beginning, please insert your flash drive (or memory stick) and create a folder for our course; "Electrical 1 – DC Theory" (if you don't have one already). This is where you will save your lab data for this and all future labs and in the formats shown below.

1. **Simulating the Circuit**
    1.1 Log on to the workstation computer, locate and run the MultiSim software by clicking on Start → All Programs → National Instruments → Circuit Design Suite 11.0 → MultiSim.
    1.2 Bring in a 15 VDC battery and connect it's negative terminal to a ground point.
    1.3 Bring in a 100 Ω resistor and connect it to an Ohmmeter.
    1.4 Turn the "Power On" and "Measure" (and record) the resistance of the resistor. $R_{R1} = $ _____
    1.5 Turn the "Power Off" and "build" the simple circuit in the pre-lab "Preparation".
    1.6 Turn the "Power" back "On" and "Measure" (and record) the voltage across the resistor. $V_{R1} = $ _____
    1.7 "Measure" and record the current through the resistor. $I_{R1} = $ _____
    1.8 "Measure" and record the power dissipated by the resistor. $P_{R1} = $ _____
    1.9 Create a folder on your flash drive or your FOL locker titled with our course code. Save the simulation in the following file format.

    Lab 5 - Introduction Circuit <u>Simulation</u> – (Today's Date) - (Your Full Name) - (Your Course and Section Number)

    1.10 Go back to MultiSim and show the 3D breadboard view of your circuit. Place and connect all the components (except the meters) on the breadboard.
    1.11 Take a screen shot of the breadboard by hitting ALT + PrtSc simultaneously.
    1.12 Open MsPaint by clicking on Start → All Programs → Accessories → Paint.
    1.13 Paste the "screen shot" image in to MsPaint and save it in ".jpeg" format using the following file structure:

    Lab 5 - Introduction Circuit <u>3D Image</u> – (Today's Date) - (Your Full Name) - (Your Course and Section Number)

    1.14 In the space provided below, and using your component stencil, please redraw the circuit found in the Pre-Lab but change the voltage source (E_1) to 9 VDC and the resistance of R_1 to 2.2 kΩ. Also, please calculate what you think you should measure for V_{R1}, I_{R1} and P_{R1} with the new circuit component values.

$V_{R1} = $ _____, $I_{R1} = $ _____, $P_{R1} = $ _____

1.15 Go back to MultiSim and change the voltage source (E_1) to 9 VDC and the resistance of R_1 to 2.2 kΩ.

1.16 Turn the "Power" back "On", measure and record the values for R_{R1}, V_{R1}, I_{R1} and P_{R1}.

R_{R1} = _____, V_{R1} = _____, I_{R1} = _____, P_{R1} = _____

1.17 Resave the simulation to your flash drive or FOL locker in the following file format.

Lab 5 - Introduction Circuit Image – (Today's Date) - (Your Full Name) - (Your Course and Section Number) – Rev A. *It is always good practice to record the revision level in the title.*

1.18 Exit MultiSim, logoff the station and clean up your work station.

1.19 Please print off the original circuit simulation and the 3D breadboard layout and attach them (either with glue, tape or staples) to this lab in the space provided below. Please be sure to shrink (or resize) the images as needed so that they fit appropriately. Also be sure to cut and attach the images so that they look neat and professional.

Image 5.1.1 – Original Circuit Simulation

Image 5.1.2 – 3D Breadboard Layout

ANALYSIS/OBSERVATIONS:

1) Please compare (in detail) the data recorded in step 1.6 (V_{R1}, I_{R1} and P_{R1}) with the measurements made on this same circuit in Lab 3. Calculate the percent difference between this week's nominal values and Lab 3's measured values below.

2) Have your neighbor grade your pre-lab and above calculations based on our grading structure. Were they what you expected? If not, why?

3) Make a detailed observation to the value (or usefulness) of using simulation software as a "circuit calculator" for verifying manual calculations or as a means of validating prototype circuits.

4) Make an observation as to the speed of solving unknown circuit quantites using MultiSim as opposed to manual calculation and actually building the circuit and taking measurements.

5) What disadvantages does <u>solely</u> relying on simulation results pose for circuit design?

CONCLUSION:

Please describe in detail which lab objectives you met (if any) and how they were achieved.

After your lab has been signed off and you have cleaned up your work station, please go around to see if others need help and assist (not distract) them. Remember, we assist by making observations and asking questions with our hands behind our backs.

Grade Breakdown Structure

(Refer to your Weekly Lab Rubric or the Sample Rubric posted in your lab manual for more detail.)

	Lab: Introduction to MultiSim	Score				
1	Section 1 – Preparation		3	2	1	0
2	Section 2 – Experimentation		3	2	1	0
3	Section 3 – Analysis, Conclusion and Professionalism	4	3	2	1	0
Notes/Comments:		**Total**				
		Teacher's Signature (above)				
		Name				
		Date				

DC Series Circuits, Ohm's Law, Joule's Law and KVL

Name: _____   Course and Section: _____

Partner: _____   Date: _____

PURPOSE:

The purpose of this lab is to become familiar with the following:
1. To build, troubleshoot and take measurements in a series circuit.
2. Verify Ohm's and Joule's Laws by comparing calculated, simulated and measured values.
3. Verify Kirchhoff's Voltage Law (KVL) in an open circuit.
4. Use a digital multi-meter (DMM) to measure resistance, current and voltage.
5. To learn to use the dual variable voltage power supplies at the lab test stations.

EQUIPMENT:

1. Your tool and component kits (see your CIS on FOL)
2. Your PPE (untinted/untreated, CSA approved safety glasses with side shields)
3. A breadboard, jumper wires and alligator leads
4. Your DMM (Digital Multi-Meter – MTP 2327)
5. Your calculator (Sharp EL-516)
6. Various coloured pencil crayons
7. Resistors: 100 Ω (1), 330 Ω (1) and 470 Ω (1)
8. Potentiometers: 10 kΩ Trim Potentiometer

PREPARATION: *For full marks, please show **all** your work when performing calculations.*

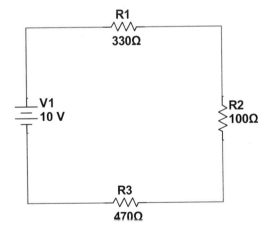

1) In the space provided below, determine all the required quantities shown in Table 6.0.1, write your final answers in Table 6.0.1 and write the root KVL equation for the circuit below Table 6.0.1.

2) Use Multi-Sim and "measure I_T, V_{R1}, V_{R2}, V_{R3}, P_{R1}, P_{R2} and P_{R3}. Save a screen shot of your simulated circuit, print it off and attach it to your pre-lab.

3) On the breadboard shown below, show exactly how you would connect all the components and instruments (a wiring diagram) to accurately measure I_T and V_{R3}.

Please Note: *In addition to the items listed in the rubric, this pre-lab will be worth all 3 of the lab "preparation" marks. 1 Mark for each of the above items. Remember to use the correct algebraic manipulation of the equations (with variables and sub-scripts) then number substitution and final*

© 2016

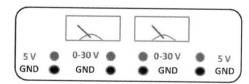

Louis Jraige

answer in standard engineering notation (with prefixes) and the proper units. When sketching the wiring diagram, please use the appropriate standards and conventions shown. Also, be sure to use only straight (or 90° bent) lines created with a ruler and connection nodes where appropriate for all connections.

Pre-Lab Calculations:

Table 6.0.1

Calculated	Current	Voltage	Power
Supply			
R1			
R2			
R3			
RT			
KVL Root Equation			

Be sure to use the correct DMM terminals, to show the correct orientation of the selector switch on the DMM body and to indicate the meter reading on the DMM's LCD screen as well.

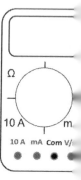

Please use the following conventions:

Red wires for (+)

Black wires for (-).

Blue wires for jumpers.

Grey —▭— for resistors.

Black ● for node connections.

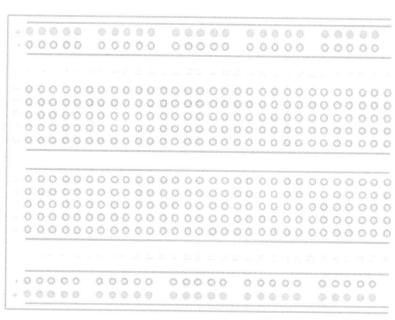

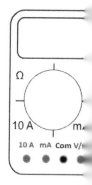

Image 6.0.1 – Original Circuit Simulation
(Powered and with all Instruments Displaying their Readings Simultaneously)

Louis Jraige

DESIGN INTENT:

In this lab we will investigate series circuits and validate Kirchhoff's Voltage Law and Joule's Power Law by examining the effect on the circuit element voltage drops when R_2 is open and then shorted out of the circuit.

A few things we should note when building and testing circuits. First, when building any circuit, please try and use as few jumpers as possible while still building your circuit neatly. The less you have on your board, the less you have to troubleshoot when your circuit doesn't work. When setting up the source voltage, be sure to set it as closely to the desired voltage as possible. Getting it "close enough" is not "good enough". Be sure to measure and record all the required values (E_{S1}, R_T, I_T, P_T, etc.). You should always compare your measurements with your pre-lab data.

In this lab, we will be investigating the impact the two "extreme" values a resistor can be (short; 0Ω and open $\infty\Omega$), has on a circuit. Keep in mind that every other resistance value will fall between these two "extreme" values. We can investigate the impact a varying resistor has on the circuit.

BACKGROUND DATA:

TEXTBOOK REFERENCE:

PROCEDURE:

1. **Ohm's Law, Power Law and Kirchhoff's Voltage Law**

   1.1 Locate all the resistors required for this lab, measure their resistances and record their values in Table 6.1.1.

   1.2 Using your resistors and breadboard, build the circuit shown in the Lab Preparation section, measure the total circuit resistance and record their value in Table 6.1.1.

   1.3 Use your DMM to measure the terminal voltage and set your power supply 10 VDC.

   1.4 Turn off your power supply and set the Current (CC) potentiometer is set to 1/3 of a turn CW.

   1.5 Connect the power supply to your circuit and switch the power supply on.

   1.6 Use the fine adjustment potentiometer to "tweak" the power supply voltage to 10 VDC and record the source voltage in Table 6.1.1.

   1.7 Turn off your power supply.

   1.8 Set your DMM to its 200 mA range, attach your leads to the appropriate sockets and connect it between the power supply and R_1 such that you read a positive current for I_T.

   1.9 Switch the power supply on.

   1.10 Use the most appropriate range (or scale) for the most accurate reading (without exceeding the scales range) and record your circuit current in Table 6.1.1.

   1.11 Shut the power supply off and reconnect your circuit directly to the power supply.

   1.12 Reset your DMM to measure DC voltage (leads in the right sockets) and set it to the 20 VDC scale.

   1.13 Turn on the power supply, measure the voltage drops across each of the circuit resistances by placing the DMM leads in parallel with each element and record their values in Table 6.1.1.

   1.14 Turn off your power supply and calculate how much power each resistor is using and how much power is being supplied to the circuit in the space provided below.

2. Testing Ohm's Law, Joule's Law and KVL

2.1 Turn off your power supply and remove R_2 from the circuit by giving the circuit current a low resistance path (of 0 Ω) around it; a short circuit by placing a jumper across R_2.

2.2 Turn your power supply back on, measure the voltage drops across each resistor (including the new R_2 of 0 Ω), record their values in Table 6.2.1 and turn off your power supply.

2.3 Set your DMM to its 200 mA range, attach your leads to the appropriate sockets and connect it between the power supply and R_1 such that you read a positive current.

2.4 Connect the power supply to your circuit and switch the power supply on.

2.5 Use the most appropriate range (or scale) for the most accurate reading (without exceeding the scales range) and record your circuit current in Table 6.2.1.

2.6 Turn off your power supply and remove the "short" across R_2 and R_2 itself; so that now the "new" value of "R_2" is ∞ Ω.

2.7 Turn on the power supply and retake and record all the resistance, current and voltage readings with the new "R_2" values in Table 6.2.2. Be careful how you connect your DMM. You do not want to accidentally "modify" the circuit when connecting your instrument.

2.8 Turn off the power supply and calculate how much power each resistor (including the new R_2 values at 0 Ω and ∞ Ω) used. Be sure to show _all_ your work in the space provided below.

3. **Testing Ohm's Law, Joule's Law and KVL** *(Optional – Time Permitting)*

3.1 With the power supply off, replace R_2 with a variable resistance; a 10 kΩ trim potentiometer. Connect the trim potentiometer as a rheostat by connecting only one of the end terminals and the wiper arm to the circuit and set the potentiometer to its lowest setting (0 Ω).

3.2 Create a scale on the potentiometer body with a pencil. Mark the 0%, 25%, 50%, 75 % and 100 % deflection points on the potentiometer body with a pencil. The easiest way to do this is to mark the 0% and then the 100% points. Then, by eye, find and mark the 50% point. Finally, and again by eye, mark the 25% and 75% marks. Be sure to measure the resistance of the potentiometer at each of the points and record them in Table 6.3.1.

3.3 Turn your power supply back on, measure the voltage drop across the new R_2 values at each point in the rotation of the wiper arm, record their values in Table 6.3.1 and turn off your power supply.

3.4 Set your DMM to its 200 mA range, attach your leads to the appropriate sockets and connect it between the power supply and R_1 such that you read a positive current.

3.5 Turn on the power supply and retake all the new R_2 values at each point in the rotation of the wiper arm and record them in Table 6.3.1. Be careful how you connect your DMM. You do not want to accidentally "modify" the circuit when connecting your instrument.

3.6 Turn off the power supply and calculate how much power each resistor (including each of the new R_2 values) used. Be sure to show <u>all</u> your work in the space provided below.

Louis Jraige

ANALYSIS/OBSERVATIONS:

Please use the space below to capture/record your data/information or to answer questions. For full marks, please show **_all_** your work when performing calculations.

Table 6.1.1

Original	Resistance	Current	Voltage	Power
Total				
R_1				
R_2				
R_3				

Table 6.2.1

R_2 Shorted	Resistance	Current	Voltage	Power
Total				
R_1				
R_2 (the resistor)				
R_2 (the jumper)				
R_3				

Table 6.2.2

R$_2$ Open	Resistance	Current	Voltage	Power
Total				
R$_1$				
R$_2$ (the resistor)		0 mA		
R$_2$ (the space)	∞ Ω	0 mA		
R$_3$				

Table 6.3.1

R$_2$ Variable	Resistance	Current	Voltage	Power
R$_2$ @ 0%				
R$_2$ @ 25%				
R$_2$ @ 50%				
R$_2$ @ 75%				
R$_2$ @ 100%				

1) Refer to Tables 6.1.1 and 6.2.1. Are the voltage, current and power readings what you would expect to see from that circuit configuration? Please explain why or why not in detail.

2) Refer to Tables 6.1.1 and 6.3.1. Are the voltage, current and power readings what you would expect to see from that circuit configuration? Please explain why or why not in detail.

3) Refer to Tables 6.2.1 and 6.3.1. Are the voltage, current and power readings what you would expect to see from that circuit configuration? Please explain why or why not in detail.

4) Have a friend grade the calculations from your analysis section and grade your work according to our grading structure while you grade theirs. Have your friend fill out the information below.

Name:_____   Date:_____   Grade:_____

CONCLUSION:

Please describe in detail which lab objectives you met (if any) and how they were achieved.

After your lab has been signed off and you have cleaned up your work station, please go around to see if others need help and assist (not distract) them. Remember, we assist by making observations and asking questions with our hands behind our backs.

Grade Breakdown Structure
(Refer to your Weekly Lab Rubric or the Sample Rubric posted in your lab manual for more detail.)

	Lab: DC Series Circuits, Ohm's Law, Joule's Law and KVL	Score				
1	Section 1 – Preparation		3	2	1	0
2	Section 2 – Experimentation		3	2	1	0
3	Section 3 – Analysis, Conclusion and Professionalism	4	3	2	1	0
Notes/Comments:		**Total**				
		Teacher's Signature (above)				
		Name				
		Date				

© 2016

Louis Jraige

DC Parallel Circuits, Ohm's Law, Joule's Law and KCL

Name: _____   Course and Section: _____

Partner: _____   Date: _____

PURPOSE:

The purpose of this lab is to become familiar with the following:
1. To build, troubleshoot and take measurements in a parallel circuit.
2. Verify Ohm's and Joule's Laws by comparing calculated, simulated and measured values.
3. Verify Kirchhoff's Current Law (KCL) in an open circuit.
4. Use a digital multi-meter (DMM) to measure resistance, current and voltage.
5. To learn to use the dual variable voltage power supplies at the lab test stations.

EQUIPMENT:

1. Your tool and component kits (see your CIS on FOL)
2. Your PPE (untinted/untreated, CSA approved safety glasses with side shields)
3. A breadboard, jumper wires and alligator leads
4. Your DMM (Digital Multi-Meter – MTP 2327)
5. Your calculator (Sharp EL-516)
6. Various coloured pencil crayons
7. Resistors: 100 Ω (5 Watt Power Resistor) (1), 1 kΩ (1) and 1 MΩ (1)

PREPARATION: *For full marks, please show **all** your work when performing calculations.*

1) In the space provided below, determine all the required quantities shown in Table 7.0.1, write your final answers in Table 7.0.1 and write the root KCL equation for the circuit below Table 7.0.1.

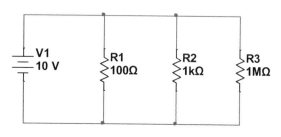

2) Use Multi-Sim and "measure I_T, I_{R1}, I_{R2}, I_{R3}, P_{R1}, P_{R2} and P_{R3}. Save a screen shot of your simulated circuit, print it off and attach it to your pre-lab.

3) On the breadboard shown below, show exactly how you would connect all the components and instruments (wiring diagram) to accurately measure I_T and I_{R2}.

__Please Note:__ In addition to the items listed in the rubric, this pre-lab will be worth all 3 of the lab "preparation" marks. 1 Mark for each of the above items. Remember to use the correct algebraic manipulation of the equations (with variables and sub-scripts) then number substitution and final answer in standard engineering notation (with prefixes) and the proper units. When sketching the *wiring diagram, please use the standards and conventions shown. Also, be sure to use only straight (or 90° bent) lines created with a ruler and connection nodes where appropriate for all connections.*

Pre-Lab Calculations:

Table 7.0.1

Calculated	Current	Voltage	Power
Supply			
R1			
R2			
R3			
RT			
KCL Root Equation			

Be sure to use the correct DMM terminals, to show the correct orientation of the selector switch on the DMM body and to indicate the meter reading on the DMM's LCD screen as well.

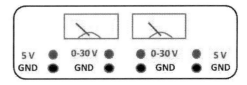

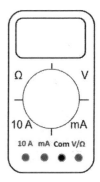

Please use the following conventions:

Red wires for (+)

Black wires for (-).

Blue wires for jumpers.

Grey ⊏▭⊐ for resistors.

Black ● for node connections.

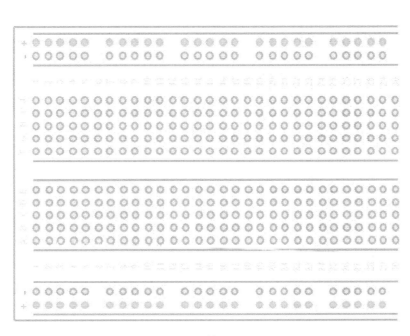

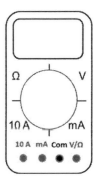

Louis Jraige

Image 7.0.1 – Original Circuit Simulation
(Powered and with all Instruments Displaying their Readings Simultaneously)

DESIGN INTENT:

In this lab we will investigate parallel circuits and validate Kirchhoff's Current Law and Joule's Power Law by examining the effect on the circuit element current draws when R_1 is open and then shorted out of the circuit.

A few things we should note when building and testing circuits. First, when building any circuit, please try and use as few jumpers as possible while still building your circuit neatly. The less you have on your board, the less you have to troubleshoot when your circuit doesn't work. When setting up the source voltage, be sure to set it as closely to the desired voltage as possible. Getting it "close enough" is not "good enough". Be sure to measure and record all the required values (E_{S1}, R_T, I_T, P_T, etc.). You should always compare your measurements with your pre-lab data.

In this lab, we will be investigating the impact the two "extreme" values a resistor can be (short; 0Ω and open $\infty\Omega$), has on a circuit. Keep in mind that every other resistance value will fall between these two "extreme" values.

BACKGROUND DATA:

TEXTBOOK REFERENCE:

Louis Jraige

PROCEDURE:

1. **Ohm's Law, Power Law and Kirchhoff's Current Law**
    1.1 Locate all the resistors required for this lab, measure their resistances and record their values in Table 7.1.1.
    1.2 Using your resistors and breadboard, build the circuit shown in the Lab Preparation section, measure the total circuit resistance and record their value in Table 7.1.1.
    1.3 Use your DMM to measure the terminal voltage and set your power supply 10 VDC.
    1.4 Turn off your power supply and set the Current (CC) potentiometer is set to 1/3 of a turn CW.
    1.5 Connect the power supply to your circuit and switch the power supply on.
    1.6 Use the fine adjustment potentiometer to "tweak" the power supply voltage to 10 VDC and record the source voltage in Table 7.1.1.
    1.7 Measure the voltage drop across each of the resistors and record their values in Table 7.1.1.
    1.8 Turn off your power supply.
    1.9 Set your DMM to its 200 mA range, attach your leads to the appropriate sockets and connect it in series with R_1 such that you read a positive current for I_T.
    1.10 Switch the power supply on.
    1.11 Use the most appropriate range (or scale) for the most accurate reading (without exceeding the scales range) and record your circuit current in Table 7.1.1.
    1.12 Shut the power supply off, remove your DMM, and reconnect the circuit. Now, connect your DMM to measure I_{R1}, turn the power supply on and record the current in Table 7.1.1.
    1.13 Repeat step 1.12 for I_{R2} and I_{R3}.
    1.14 Shut the power supply off, remove your DMM, and reconnect the original circuit.
    1.15 Turn off your power supply and calculate how much power each resistor is using and how much power is being supplied to the circuit in the space provided below.

© 2016

52

2. Testing Ohm's Law, Joule's Law and KCL *(with R₁ Shorted; No Resistance or essentially 0 Ω)*

2.1 Turn off your power supply, remove R_1 from the circuit by giving the circuit current a low resistance path (of 0 Ω) around it; a short circuit by placing a jumper across R_1.

2.2 **Set the Current (CC) potentiometer is set to 1/3 of a turn <u>CW</u>.** *This step is very important so as not to overwork the power supply and draw so much current that the jumpers overheat.*

2.3 Turn your power supply back on, measure the voltage drops across each resistor, record their values in Table 7.2.1 and then turn off your power supply.

2.4 Set your DMM to its 200 mA range, attach your leads to the appropriate sockets and connect it in series with R_1 such that you read a positive current for I_{R1}.

2.5 Switch the power supply on.

2.6 Use the most appropriate range (or scale) for the most accurate reading (without exceeding the scales range) and record your circuit current in Table 7.2.1.

2.7 Shut the power supply off, remove your DMM, and reconnect the circuit.

2.8 Repeat steps 2.4 to 2.7 but for I_{R2} and I_{R3}.

2.9 Set your DMM to its **10 A range**, attach your leads to the appropriate sockets and connect it between the power supply and the circuit such that you read a positive current for I_T. *Remember, you cannot use the 10 A range for too long a time without damaging your DMM. The power supply should be on for **no more than 10 seconds** while taking a current reading on the 10 A range.*

2.10 Switch the power supply on and very quickly, take the current reading for I_T (total circuit current) and then shut the power supply off. Record your measurement in Table 7.2.1.

2.11 Connect your DMM to measure the series current in the "short" or "jumper" (between the power supply and the short or jumper) such that you read a positive current for I_{Short}. *Remember, you cannot use the 10 A range for too long a time without damaging your DMM. The power supply should be on for **no more than 10 seconds** while taking a current reading on the 10 A range.*

2.12 Switch the power supply on and very quickly, take the current reading for I_{Short} and then shut the power supply off. Record your measurement in Table 7.2.1.

2.13 With the power supply off, remove your DMM and jumper and reconnect the original circuit.

2.14 Calculate how much power each resistor is using and how much power is being supplied to the circuit in the space provided below.

Louis Jraige

3. Testing Ohm's Law, Joule's Law and KCL *(R₁ Open; Essentially Infinite Resistance or ∞ Ω)*

3.1 Turn off your power supply and replace R_1 with a large resistance (of ∞ Ω); an open circuit by removing R_1 from the circuit.

3.2 Turn your power supply back on, measure the voltage drops across each resistor (including the new R_1 of ∞ Ω), record their values in Table 7.3.1 and then turn off your power supply.

3.3 Set your DMM to its 200 mA range, attach your leads to the appropriate sockets and connect it between the power supply and the circuit such that you read a positive current for I_T.

3.4 Switch the power supply on.

3.5 Use the most appropriate range (or scale) for the most accurate reading (without exceeding the scales range) and record your circuit current in Table 7.3.1.

3.6 Shut the power supply off, remove your DMM, and reconnect the circuit. Now, connect your DMM to measure I_{R3}, turn the power supply on and record the current in Table 7.3.1.

3.7 Repeat steps 3.4 to 3.6 for I_{R2} and I_{R1} (which should still be open). Be careful not to complete the circuit when measuring I_{R1}.

3.8 Shut the power supply off, remove your DMM, and reconnect the original circuit.

3.9 Turn off your power supply and calculate how much power each resistor is using and how much power is being supplied to the circuit in the space provided below.

ANALYSIS/OBSERVATIONS:

Please use the space below to capture/record your data/information or to answer questions. For full marks, please show **_all_** your work when performing calculations.

Table 7.1.1

Measured	Resistance	Current	Voltage	Power
Total				
R1				
R2				
R3				

Table 7.2.1

R_1 Shorted	Resistance	Current	Voltage	Power
Total				
R_1 (the resistor)				
R_1 (the jumper)				
R_2				
R_3				

Table 7.3.1

R_1 Open	Resistance	Current	Voltage	Power
Total				
R_1 (the resistor)		0 mA		
R_1 (the jumper)	$\infty \ \Omega$	0 mA		
R_2				
R_3				

Louis Jraige

1) Refer to Tables 7.1.1 and 7.2.1. Are the voltage, current and power readings what you would expect to see from that circuit configuration? Please explain why or why not in detail.

2) Refer to Tables 7.1.1 and 7.3.1. Are the voltage, current and power readings what you would expect to see from that circuit configuration? Please explain why or why not in detail.

3) Refer to Tables 7.2.1 and 7.3.1. Are the voltage, current and power readings what you would expect to see from that circuit configuration? Please explain why or why not in detail.

4) Have a friend grade the calculations from your analysis section and grade your work according to our grading structure while you grade theirs. Have your friend fill out the information below.

Name:_____ Date:_____ Grade:_____

CONCLUSION:

Please describe in detail which lab objectives you met (if any) and how they were achieved.

After your lab has been signed off and you have cleaned up your work station, please go around to see if others need help and assist (not distract) them. Remember, we assist by making observations and asking questions with our hands behind our backs.

Grade Breakdown Structure

(Refer to your Weekly Lab Rubric or the Sample Rubric posted in your lab manual for more detail.)

	Lab: DC Parallel Circuits, Ohm's Law, Joule's Law and KCL	Score				
1	Section 1 – Preparation		3	2	1	0
2	Section 2 – Experimentation		3	2	1	0
3	Section 3 – Analysis, Conclusion and Professionalism	4	3	2	1	0
Notes/Comments:		**Total**				
		Teacher's Signature (above)				
		Name				
		Date				

© 2016

Louis Jraige

DC Combination Circuits, Ohm's Law, Joule's Law, KVL, KCL, VDR and CDR

Name: _____   Course and Section: _____

Partner: _____   Date: _____

PURPOSE:

The purpose of this lab is to become familiar with the following:
1. To build, troubleshoot and take measurements in a series/parallel combination circuit.
2. Verify Ohm's and Joule's Laws by comparing calculated, simulated and measured values.
3. Use the "Reduce and Return" method to reinforce "Equivalent Circuit" concepts for circuit analysis.
4. Apply Ohm's Law (OL), the Joule's Law (JL), Kirchhoff's Voltage Law (KVL) and Kirchhoff's Current Law (KCL), the Voltage Divider Rule (VDR) and the Current Divider Rule (CDR) in a combination circuit.
5. Use a digital multi-meter (DMM) to measure resistance, current and voltage.
6. To learn to use the dual variable voltage power supplies at the lab test stations.

EQUIPMENT:

1. Your tool and component kits (see your CIS on FOL)
2. Your PPE (untinted/untreated, CSA approved safety glasses with side shields)
3. A breadboard, jumper wires and alligator leads
4. Your DMM (Digital Multi-Meter – MTP 2327)
5. Your calculator (Sharp EL-516)
6. Various coloured pencil crayons
7. Resistors: 2 kΩ (1), 4.7 kΩ (2), 5.6 kΩ (1) and 10 kΩ (1)

PREPARATION: *For full marks, please show **all** your work when performing calculations. Give all answers in engineering notation with prefixes and rounded to three decimals.*

1) On the next page, use the "Reduce and Return" method to determine all the required quantities shown and draw the simplified equivalent circuit in the space provided below:

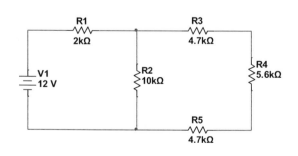
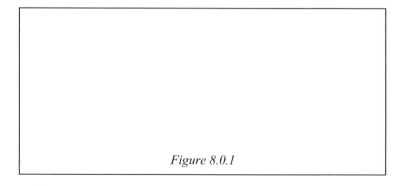

Figure 8.0.1

**Please Note:** _In addition to the items listed in the rubric, this pre-lab will be worth all 3 of the lab "preparation" marks; 1 mark for Sections 2, 3 and 4. Remember to use the correct algebraic manipulation of the equations (with variables and sub-scripts) then number substitution and final answer in standard engineering notation (with prefixes) and the proper units. When sketching the wiring diagram, please use the appropriate standards and conventions shown._

Table 5.0.1

Calculated	Current	Voltage	Power
Supply			
R_1			
R_2			
R_3			
R_4			
R_5			
R_T			

Louis Jraige

2) *Please re-solve the following using the indicated methods below:*

   a. *Use the product over sum method to determine $R_{T'}$ (R_2 // $R_{3,4,5}$) and use the reciprocal of reciprocals method to calculate the total circuit resistance.*

   b. *Use the VDR to determine V_{R1}:*

   c. *Use KVL to determine V_{R2}:*

   d. *Use OL to determine I_T:*

   e. *Use the CDR to determine I_{R2}:*

   f. *Use KCL to determine I_{R3}:*

   g. *Use the JL to determine P_{R4}:*

3) *Please use Multi-Sim to simulate the circuit and use the DMMs to show V_{R1}, V_{R2}, I_T, I_{R1}, P_{R3} and P_{R4}. Please take a "screen shot" of your circuit and DMMs (showing their values simultaneously), save it as a .jpeg, print it off and attach it to your pre-lab.*

Image 8.0.1 – Original Circuit Simulation
(Powered and with all Instruments Displaying their Readings Simultaneously)

Louis Jraige

4) *On the breadboard shown below, neatly and clearly show exactly how you would connect all the components and instruments (wiring diagram) to accurately measure V_{R1}, V_{R2}, V_{R3}, I_{R1}, I_{R2} and I_{R3}. Be sure to maximize your available space and that your work is easy to read and follow using only straight (or 90° bent) lines created with a ruler and connection nodes.*

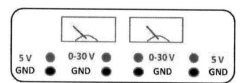

Be sure to use the correct DMM terminals, to show the correct orientation of the selector switch on the DMM body and to indicate the meter reading on the DMM's LCD screen as well.

Please use the following conventions:

Red wires for (+)

Black wires for (-).

Blue wires for jumpers.

Grey for resistors.

Black for node connections.

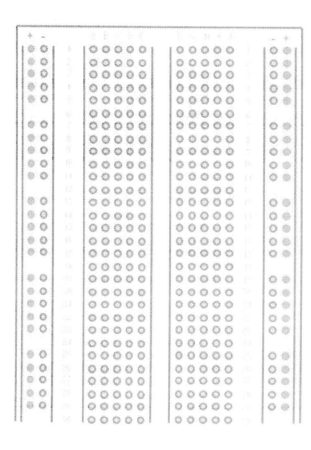

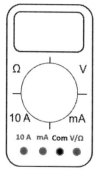

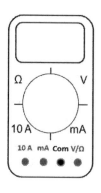

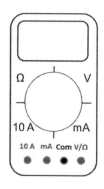

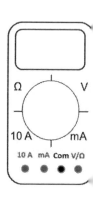

DESIGN INTENT:

In this lab we will investigate combination (series/parallel) circuits to validate "The Big 6"; OL (Ohms Law), KVL (Kirchhoff's Voltage Law), KCL (Kirchhoff's Current Law), JL or JPL (Joule's Power Law), VDR (Voltage Divider Rule) and the CDR (Current Divider Rule).

BACKGROUND DATA:

TEXTBOOK REFERENCE:

PROCEDURE:

1. **Ohm's Law, Joule's Law and Kirchhoff's Voltage Law**

    1.1 Locate all the resistors required for this lab, measure their resistances and record their values in Table 8.1.1.

    1.2 Using your resistors and breadboard, build the circuit shown in the Lab Preparation section, measure the total circuit resistance and record their value in Table 8.1.1.

    1.3 Use your DMM to measure the terminal voltage and set your power supply 12 VDC and turn off your power supply. Please remember when measuring the voltage across an element, the DMM must be connected in parallel with that element.

    1.4 Connect the power supply to your circuit and switch the power supply on.

    1.5 Use the fine adjustment potentiometer to "tweak" the power supply voltage to 12 VDC and record the source voltage in Table 8.1.1.

    1.6 Measure the voltage drop across each of the resistors and record their values in Table 8.1.1.

    1.7 Attach your DMM leads to the appropriate sockets to measure current, set your DMM to the most appropriate ranges, measure the current through each resistor and record their values in Table 8.1.1. Remember; never modify a circuit with the power on. Be sure to turn off the power supply before removing any of the components and connecting the DMM for current measurements. Also, please remember when measuring the current through an element, the DMM must be connected in series with that element.

    1.8 Turn off your power supply and calculate how much power each resistor is using and how much power was being supplied to the circuit.

ANALYSIS/OBSERVATIONS:

Please use the space below to capture/record your data/information or to answer questions. For full marks, please show **_all_** your work when performing calculations.

Table 8.1.1

Measured	Resistance	Current	Voltage	Power
Total				
R_1				
R_2				
R_3				
R_4				
R_5				

1) Please use your measured, calculated and simulated data and calculate the percent difference between V_{R1}, I_T and P_{R4}. Use your calculated values as the nominal values.

2) Please explain in detail why the DMM must be connected "across" the resistor (in parallel) when measuring voltage and connected "in-line" with the resistor (in series) when measuring current. Please refer to the DMM's internal resistance and the Voltage/Current Divider Rules.

Louis Jraige

CONCLUSION:

Please describe in detail which lab objectives you met (if any) and how they were achieved.

After your lab has been signed off and you have cleaned up your work station, please go around to see if others need help and assist (not distract) them. Remember, we assist by making observations and asking questions with our hands behind our backs.

Grade Breakdown Structure
(Refer to your Weekly Lab Rubric or the Sample Rubric posted in your lab manual for more detail.)

	Lab: DC Comb. Circuits, OL, JL, KVL, KCL, VDR and CDR	Score				
1	Section 1 – Preparation	3		2	1	0
2	Section 2 – Experimentation	3		2	1	0
3	Section 3 – Analysis, Conclusion and Professionalism	4	3	2	1	0
Notes/Comments:		**Total**				
		Teacher's Signature (above)				
		Name				
		Date				

Louis Jraige

DC Superposition Theorem and Mesh Loop Analysis

Name: _____   Course and Section: _____

Partner: _____   Date: _____

PURPOSE:

The purpose of this lab is to become familiar with the following:
1. Validate the Superposition theorem by comparing calculated, simulated and measured values.
2. Use a digital multi-meter (DMM) to measure resistance, current and voltage.
3. Use MultiSim to validate measured and calculated values.
4. To use the dual variable voltage power supplies at the lab test stations for series voltage connections.

EQUIPMENT:

1. Your tool and component kits (see your CIS on FOL)
2. Your PPE (untinted/untreated, CSA approved safety glasses with side shields)
3. A breadboard, jumper wires and alligator leads
4. Your DMM (Digital Multi-Meter – MTP 2327)
5. Your calculator (Sharp EL-516)
6. Various coloured pencil crayons
7. Resistors: 1.2 kΩ (1), 2.2 kΩ (1) and 3.3 kΩ (1)

PREPARATION: *For full marks, please show **all** your work when performing calculations. Give all answers in engineering notation with prefixes and rounded to three decimals.*

Please Note: *In addition to the items listed in the rubric, this pre-lab will be worth all 3 of the lab "preparation" marks; 1 mark for Sections 1, 2 and (3 and 4 together). Remember to use the correct algebraic manipulation of the equations (with variables and sub-scripts) then number substitution and final answer in standard engineering notation (with prefixes) and the proper units. When sketching the wiring diagram, please use the appropriate standards and conventions shown.*

1) *Use superposition to solve for I_{R1}, I_{R2} and I_{R3} for the circuit shown below. Use I_{R1}, I_{R2} and I_{R3} to determine V_{R1}, V_{R2}, V_{R3}, P_{R1}, P_{R2} and P_{R3}.*

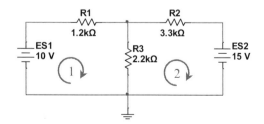

Using E_{S1} Only:

Figure 9.0.1 – Circuit Using E_{S1} Only

Using E_{S2} Only:

Figure 9.0.2 – Circuit Using E_{S2} Only

Louis Jraige

Using Both E_{S1} and E_{S2}:

2) *Solve for I_{R1}, I_{R2} and I_{R3} using* **Mesh Loops (General Approach)***. Remember to show all your work. Please write your solution as if this were a homework or term test problem. Remember to show all your algebraic manipulation with variables. Number substitution should be your second last step and express your final answer in engineering notation rounded to 3 decimals.*

Louis Jraige

3) *Solve for I_{R1}, I_{R2} and I_{R3} using* **Node Voltages (General Approach)**. *Remember to show all your work. Please write your solution as if this were a homework or term test problem. Remember to show all your algebraic manipulation with variables. Number substitution should be your second last step and express your final answer in engineering notation rounded to 3 decimals.*

4) Solve for I_{R1}, I_{R2} and I_{R3} using **Mesh Loops (Format Approach)**. Remember to show all your work. Please write your solution as if this were a homework or term test problem. Remember to show all your algebraic manipulation with variables. Number substitution should be your second last step and express your final answer in engineering notation rounded to 3 decimals.

5) Solve for I_{R1}, I_{R2} and I_{R3} using **Node Voltage (Format Approach)**. Remember to show all your work. Please write your solution as if this were a homework or term test problem. Remember to show all your algebraic manipulation with variables. Number substitution should be your second last step and express your final answer in engineering notation rounded to 3 decimals.

© 2016

6) *On the breadboard shown below, neatly and clearly show exactly how you would connect all the components and instruments (wiring diagram) to accurately measure I_{R1}, I_{R2} and I_{R3}. Be sure to maximize your available space and that your work is easy to read and follow using only straight (or 90° bent) lines created with a ruler and connection nodes where appropriate. Be sure to keep the DMMs in the same orientation as shown below for every "layer" of the simulation. I have started you on your way... (You're welcome! – LOL!)*

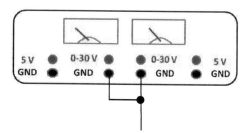

Be sure to use the correct DMM terminals, to show the correct orientation of the selector switch on the DMM body and to indicate the meter reading on the DMM's LCD screen as well.

Please use the following conventions:

Red wires for (+)

Black wires for (-).

Blue wires for jumpers.

Grey —□— for resistors.

Black ● for node connections.

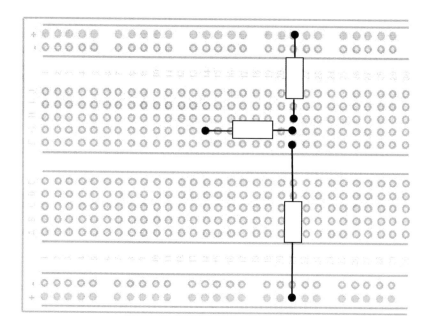

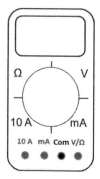

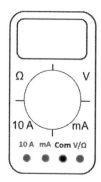

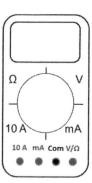

7) Use MultiSim to validate your approach and verify your answers for I_{R1}, I_{R2} and I_{R3}. Create three different circuits; 1 with E_{S1} only, 1 with E_{S2} only and 1 with both sources on the same work area. **Be sure to <u>keep the DMM connection orientation the same</u> for every "layer" (or circuit).** Please take a "screen shot" of your circuits and DMMs (showing their values simultaneously), save them as .jpegs, print them, off and attach them to your pre-lab.

*Image 9.0.3 – Using E_{S1} **Only***
(Powered and with all Instruments Displaying their Readings Simultaneously but with E_{S1} Only.)

Louis Jraige

*Image 9.0.4 – Using E_{S2} **Only***
(Powered and with all Instruments Displaying their Readings Simultaneously but with E_{S2} Only.)

*Image 9.0.5 – Original Circuit Simulations with **Both E$_{s1}$ and E$_{s2}$.***
(Powered and with all Instruments Displaying their Readings Simultaneously and with Both Sources)

PROCEDURE:

1. Superposition Theorem

1.1 Locate all the resistors required for this lab and using your breadboard, build the circuit shown in the Lab Preparation section 1.

1.2 Use your DMM to measure the terminal voltage and set the left hand variable power supply to the voltage for E_{S1} and the right hand variable power supply to the voltage for E_{S2} then turn off your power supply.

1.3 Connect the left side power supply (Slave Side - E_{S1}, and the ground terminal) to your circuit. Do not connect the right side power supply (Master Side - E_{S2}); instead install a jumper from the resistor to ground and switch the power supply on.

1.4 Attach your DMM leads to the appropriate sockets to measure current, set your DMM to the most appropriate ranges, measure the current through each resistor and record their values in Table 9.1.1. *Pay special attention to the connection orientation of the DMM. You will have to maintain that orientation for each circuit "layer". Try to keep them consistent with your Pre-Lab connection orientation.*

1.5 Shut the power supply off and connect the right side power supply (E_{S2}, and the ground terminal) to your circuit. Disconnect the left side power supply, install a jumper from the resistor to ground and switch the power supply on.

1.6 Measure the current through each of the resistors (making sure the meter is connected the way it was in the previous measurements; same orientation) and record their values in Table 9.1.1.

1.7 Turn off your power supply and calculate the current through each resistor based on steps 1.4 and 1.6 and record their values in Table 9.1.1. *Show your calculations in the space below.*

1.8 Connect both sides of the power supply (and the ground terminal) to your circuit and switch the power supply on.

1.9 Measure the current through each of the resistors (making sure the meter is connected the way it was in the previous measurements; same orientation) and record their values in Table 9.1.1.

1.10 Measure and record V_{R3}. $V_{R3} = $ _____

1.11 Compare your measured values with your Lab Preparation section 1 calculations and section 2 simulations.

ANALYSIS/OBSERVATIONS:

Please use the space below to capture/record your data/information or to answer questions.
For full marks, please show **_all_** your work when performing calculations.

Table 9.1.1

Measured	Step 1.4	Step 1.6	Step 1.7	Step 1.9	Pre-Lab S1	MultiSim S7
	I' Using ES1 Only	I'' Using ES2 Only	Calculated I_T	Measured I_T	Calculated I_T	Simulated I_T
I_{R1}						
I_{R2}						
I_{R3}						

1) In detail, please describe how your measured values compared with your calculated and simulated values.

2) Please use the data calculated in Step 1.7 and the values measured in Step1.9 to calculate the percent difference between I_{R1}, I_{R2} and I_{R3}. Use the values measured in Step1.9 as nominal.

3) Compare your calculated Mesh Loop currents to your measured currents? Based on that observation, when is it more advantageous to use Mesh Loop analysis over the Superposition?

4) Compare your calculated Mesh Loop currents to the ones calculated using Node Voltages? Based on that observation, when is it more advantageous to use Nodal analysis over the Mesh Loop analysis?

Louis Jraige

CONCLUSION:

Please describe in detail which lab objectives you met (if any) and how they were achieved.

After your lab has been signed off and you have cleaned up your work station, please go around to see if others need help and assist (not distract) them. Remember, we assist by making observations and asking questions with our hands behind our backs.

Grade Breakdown Structure

(Refer to your Weekly Lab Rubric or the Sample Rubric posted in your lab manual for more detail.)

	Lab: DC Superposition Theorem and Mesh Loop Analysis	Score				
1	Section 1 – Preparation		3	2	1	0
2	Section 2 – Experimentation		3	2	1	0
3	Section 3 – Analysis, Conclusion and Professionalism	4	3	2	1	0
Notes/Comments:		**Total**				
		Teacher's Signature (above)				
		Name				
		Date				

Thevenin's and the Maximum Power Transfer Theorems

Name: _____   Course and Section: _____

Partner: _____   Date: _____

PURPOSE:

The purpose of this lab is to become familiar with the following:
1. Changing a complex network containing several components and a voltage source into an equivalent Thevenin circuit.
2. Verify that the Thevenin circuit is equivalent to the complex network containing several components and a voltage source.
3. Apply Ohm's Law to solve the resistive circuit.
4. Use a digital multi-meter (DMM) to measure resistance and voltage.
5. To learn to use the dual variable voltage power supplies at the lab test stations.
6. To use a decade resistance box when requiring different values of resistance.
7. Determine the value of load resistance required to ensure maximum power transfer to the load.

EQUIPMENT:

1. Your tool and component kits (see your CIS on FOL)
2. Your PPE (untinted/untreated, CSA approved safety glasses with side shields)
3. A breadboard, jumper wires and alligator leads
4. Your DMM (Digital Multi-Meter – MTP 2327)
5. Your calculator (Sharp EL-516)
6. Resistors: 1.5 kΩ (1), 2.2 k Ω (1), 2.7 kΩ (1), 3.3 k Ω (1), 4.7 k Ω (1), 6.8 k Ω (1), 10 k Ω (1), 18 k Ω (1)
7. Decade Resistance box *(1 - Supplied by Fanshawe College)*

PREPARATION: *For full marks, please show **all** your work when performing calculations. Give all answers in engineering notation with prefixes and rounded to three decimals.*

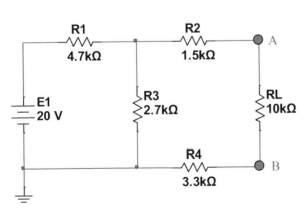

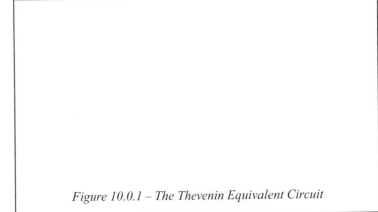

Figure 10.0.1 – The Thevenin Equivalent Circuit

Louis Jraige

1) Be sure to have read the documents labeled "The Basics of Creating and Using Graphs" (Appendix F),

2) Using Thevenin's Theorem, calculate R_{TH} and E_{TH} below. Draw the Thevenin equivalent circuit for the circuit shown in the lab preparation section including E_{TH}, R_{TH} and R_L (10 kΩ) in the box provided in the pre-lab section. Be sure your sketch is neat, clear, easy to read and follow and is _fully_ labeled

3) Using the Thevenin Equivalent circuit, please calculate V_{RL}, I_{RL} and P_{RL} for the four different load resistors (R_L (18 kΩ, 10 kΩ, 6.8 kΩ and 2.2 kΩ)) and record your values in Table 10.2.1.

Image 10.0.2
(Simulated Original Circuit and Thevenin Equivalent Circuit.)

Louis Jraige

4) *Using Norton's Theorem, calculate R_N and I_N below. Draw the Norton equivalent circuit for the circuit shown in the lab preparation section including I_N, R_N and R_L (10 kΩ) in the box provided in the pre-lab section. Be sure your sketch is neat, clear, easy to read and follow and is <u>fully</u> labeled*

5) *Using the Norton Equivalent circuit, please calculate V_{RL}, I_{RL} and P_{RL} for the four different load resistors (R_L (18 kΩ, 10 kΩ, 6.8 kΩ and 2.2 kΩ)) and record your values in Table 10.2.1.*

Image 10.0.3
(Simulated Original Circuit and Norton Equivalent Circuit.)

Louis Jraige

DESIGN INTENT:

The Thevenin circuit consists of a voltage source (Vth), which is the open-circuit voltage across the load points – in series with the equivalent internal resistance (Rth) of the circuit. This (Rth) is the resistance between the **open** load points if the internal voltage source replaced with a short circuit.

BACKGROUND DATA:

TEXTBOOK REFERENCE:

PROCEDURE:

1. **Thevenin Theorem Analysis**

   1.1 Locate all the resistors required for this lab, measure their resistances and record their values to the right of Table 10.1.1.

   1.2 Using your resistors, breadboard and power supply, build the circuit shown above in the Preparation Section and set the power supply appropriately.

   1.3 Recall that R_{TH} is equivalent resistance "looking in" from the open terminals (A and B) shown in the original circuit. To measure RTH you must set all sources to zero and then measure the total circuit resistance. Remove the source (power supply) and replace it with a short circuit. Remove the load resistor (R_L) and measure the resistance between the open-circuit load terminals (R_{TH}). Record this value in Table 10.1.1.

   1.4 Remember, E_{TH} is the voltage measured across the open terminals (A and B) shown in the original circuit. To measure E_{TH}, remove the short circuit and re-connect the power supply to the circuit. Turn the power supply on and readjust it to 20 VDC using the DMM. Measure the open-circuit load terminal voltage (V_{TH}) with your DMM. Record this value in Table 10.1.1.

   1.5 Turn off the power supply and connect the 18 kΩ load resistor between the open terminals (A and B) and turn the power supply on.

   1.6 Measure V_{RL} and record it in Table 10.2.1.

   1.7 Repeat steps 1.5 to 1.6 for the new load resistances of 10 kΩ, 6.8 kΩ and then a 2.2 kΩ load resistor, and enter those values in Table 10.2.1.

   1.8 Calculate I_{RL} for each of the load resistors under Table 10.2.1.

   1.9 Calculate the power dissipated by each of the load resistors under Table 10.2.1.

2. **Thevenin Equivalent Circuit and Maximum Power Transfer Theorem**

   2.1 Using a decade resistance box as R_{TH}, build the Thevenin equivalent circuit which was designed and calculated in the lab preparation. Adjust the decade resistance box to the value calculated for R_{TH}. Connect a decade resistance box (as R_{TH}) to the power supply and adjust the power supply to the value calculated for E_{TH}.

   2.2 Connect the 18 kΩ load resistor and measure the voltage across it (V_{RL}). Record your results in Table 10.2.1.

   2.3 Repeat step 2.2 for load resistances of 10 kΩ, 6.8 kΩ and then 2.2 kΩ loads. Record your results in Table 10.2.1.

   2.4 Calculate I_{RL} for each of the load resistors under Table 10.2.1.

   2.5 Calculate the power dissipated by each of the load resistors under Table 10.2.1.

   2.6 Redraw the Thevenin's equivalent circuit below.

Louis Jraige

ANALYSIS/OBSERVATIONS:

Please use the space below to capture/record your data/information or to answer questions. For full marks, please show **_all_** your work when performing calculations.

Table 10.1.1

	V_{TH}	R_{TH}
Calculated Values		
Measured Values		

$R_{RL\text{-}2.2k\Omega} =$ _____ , $R_1 =$ _____

$R_{RL\text{-}6.8k\Omega} =$ _____ , $R_2 =$ _____

$R_{RL\text{-}10k\Omega} =$ _____ , $R_3 =$ _____

$R_{RL\text{-}18k\Omega} =$ _____ , $R_4 =$ _____

Table 10.2.1

R_L - Load Resistance	Load Voltage (V_{RL}) *(Section 0)* *(Calculated in the Thevenin Circuit)*	Load Voltage (V_{RL}) *(Section 1)* *(Measured in the Original Circuit)*	Load Voltage (V_{RL}) *(Section 2)* *(Measured in the Thevenin Circuit)*
18 kΩ			
10 kΩ			
6.8 kΩ			
2.2 kΩ			

Section 1 Calculations:

Section 2 Calculations:

1) What did you notice about the voltage measured across each load resistor (V_{RL}) and the power dissipated by each load resistor (P_{RL}) between the original circuit (Section 1) and the Thevenin equivalent circuit (Section 2)? In detail, please describe why you think this was the case?

2) Refer to your power calculations from Section 1 and Section 2. How do they compare with what you calculated and simulated in the Pre-Lab? How far off were your measured values from your calculated power and simulated power values (as a percentage) for the 6.8 kΩ load?

3) Refer to the Maximum Power Transfer theorem and justify your power measurements from Table 10.2.1.

4) What do you think would happen to the power delivered to the 6.8 kΩ load resistor if R_3 failed open and why? How much power would actually be transferred to the load?

5) What do you think would happen to the power delivered to the 6.8 kΩ load resistor if R_3 was shorted out and why? How much power would actually be transferred to the load?

6) Refer to section 2 and plot P_{RL} vs. R_L below either manually or with MS Excel.

CONCLUSION:

Please describe in detail which lab objectives you met (if any) and how they were achieved.

After your lab has been signed off and you have cleaned up your work station, please go around to see if others need help and assist (not distract) them. Remember, we assist by making observations and asking questions with our hands behind our backs.

Grade Breakdown Structure

(Refer to your Weekly Lab Rubric or the Sample Rubric posted in your lab manual for more detail.)

	Lab: Thevenin's and the Maximum Power Transfer Theorems	Score				
1	Section 1 – Preparation		3	2	1	0
2	Section 2 – Experimentation		3	2	1	0
3	Section 3 – Analysis, Conclusion and Professionalism	4	3	2	1	0
Notes/Comments:		**Total**				
		Teacher's Signature (above)				
		Name				
		Date				

© 2016

Louis Jraige

Capacitors in DC Circuits

Name: _____   Course and Section: _____

Partner: _____   Date: _____

PURPOSE:

The purpose of this lab is to become familiar with the following:
1. Verify the basic function of a capacitor in an R-C network.
2. Use a digital multi-meter (DMM) to measure voltage and capacitance.
3. To learn to use an oscilloscope to view the voltage developed across a capacitor.

EQUIPMENT:

1. Your tool and component kits (see your CIS on FOL)
2. Your PPE (untinted/untreated, CSA approved safety glasses with side shields)
3. A breadboard, jumper wires and alligator leads
4. Your DMM (Digital Multi-Meter – MTP 2327)
5. Your calculator (Sharp EL-516)
6. A stopwatch *(or a timer that can measure seconds – most people use a mobile app for this)*
7. Resistors: 100 kΩ (1)
8. Capacitors: 100 µF (1)

PREPARATION: *For full marks, please show **all** your work when performing calculations. Give all answers in engineering notation with prefixes and rounded to three decimals.*

1) Refer to the circuit shown below and determine τ, how much time must pass before the capacitor is fully charged (t) and how much charge has been developed across the capacitor plates when it is fully charged (Q).

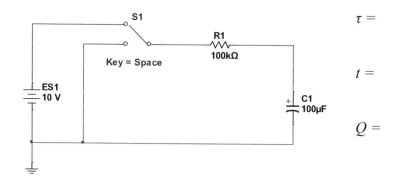

$\tau =$

$t =$

$Q =$

Please Note: *Be sure to have read the documents labeled "Capacitors and their Code Schemes" (Appendix G) and "The Oscilloscope" (Appendix J) prior to completing the pre-lab.*

2) *Refer to the circuit shown above and calculate v_c at 0τ, 1τ and 5τ for both the charge and discharge cycles. Then, plot both the charge and discharge cycles against both time and τ. Please use the scaling of 10 seconds per division. Note that the charge cycle starts at $t = 0s$ and the discharge cycle starts at $t = 70s$.*

   Please Note: *In addition to the items listed in the rubric, this pre-lab will be worth all 3 of the lab "preparation" marks; 1 Mark for each of the Sections (2, 3 and 4) of the Pre-Lab. Remember to use the correct algebraic manipulation of the equations (with variables and subscripts) then number substitution and final answer in standard engineering notation (with prefixes) and the proper units. When sketching the wiring diagram, please use the appropriate standards and conventions shown.*

   <u>*Charge Cycle Calculations:*</u>

   <u>*Discharge Cycle Calculations:*</u>

Louis Jraige

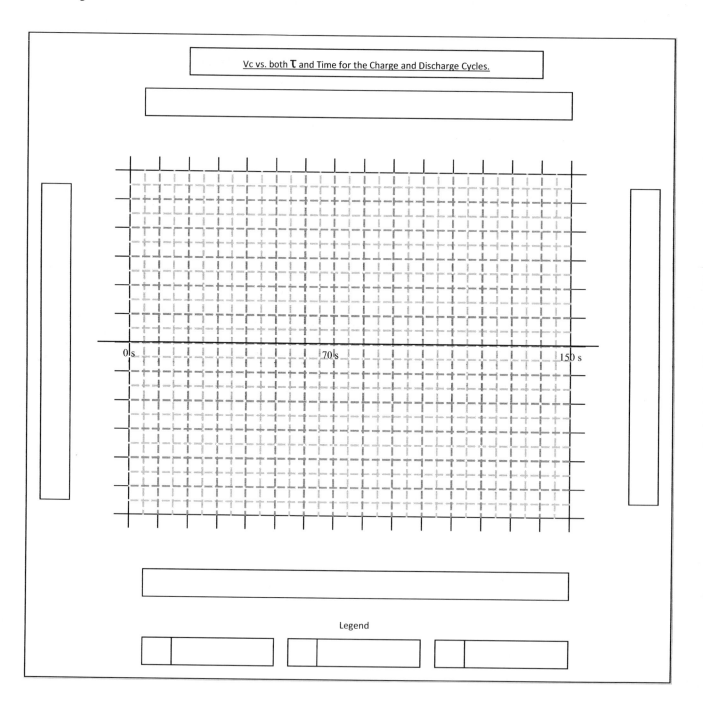

Vc vs. both τ and Time for the Charge and Discharge Cycles.

0 s   70 s   150 s

Legend

3) *Refer to the circuit shown above and calculate v_r at 0τ, 1τ and 5τ for both the charge and discharge cycles. Then, plot both the charge and discharge cycles against both time and τ. Please use the scaling of 10 seconds per division. Note that the charge cycle starts at $t = 0s$ and the discharge cycle starts at $t = 70s$.*

       <u>Please Note:</u> *In addition to the items listed in the rubric, this pre-lab will be worth all 3 of the lab "preparation" marks; 1 Mark for each of the Sections (2, 3 and 4) of the Pre-Lab. Remember to use the correct algebraic manipulation of the equations (with variables and subscripts) then number substitution and final answer in standard engineering notation (with prefixes) and the proper units. When sketching the wiring diagram, please use the appropriate standards and conventions shown.*

<u>*Charge Cycle Calculations:*</u>

<u>*Discharge Cycle Calculations:*</u>

Louis Jraige

Vr vs. both τ and Time for the Charge and Discharge Cycles.

0 s   70 s   150 s

Legend

4) *Refer to the circuit shown above and calculate i_c at 0τ, 1τ and 5τ for both the charge and discharge cycles. Then, plot both the charge and discharge cycles against both time and τ. Please use the scaling of 10 seconds per division. Note that the charge cycle starts at $t = 0s$ and the discharge cycle starts at $t = 70s$.*

*   ***Please Note:*** *In addition to the items listed in the rubric, this pre-lab will be worth all 3 of the lab "preparation" marks; 1 Mark for each of the Sections (2, 3 and 4) of the Pre-Lab. Remember to use the correct algebraic manipulation of the equations (with variables and subscripts) then number substitution and final answer in standard engineering notation (with prefixes) and the proper units. When sketching the wiring diagram, please use the appropriate standards and conventions shown.*

Charge Cycle Calculations:

Discharge Cycle Calculations:

Louis Jraige

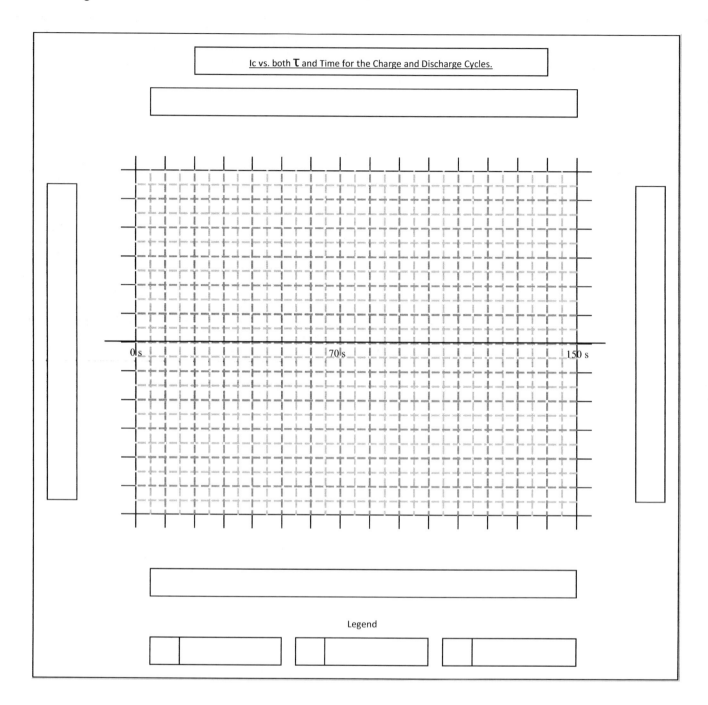

Ic vs. both τ and Time for the Charge and Discharge Cycles.

0 s   70 s   150 s

Legend

DESIGN INTENT:

In this lab, we will learn how to determine the value of a capacitor by experimentation. We will also use an oscilloscope to "view" the capacitor voltage during the charge and discharge cycles. Be sure to have read the documents labeled "The Basics of Creating and Using Graphs" (Appendix F), "Capacitors and their Code Schemes" (Appendix G) and "The Oscilloscope" (Appendix J) prior to completing the lab.

BACKGROUND DATA:

TEXTBOOK REFERENCE:

Louis Jraige

PROCEDURE:

1. Determining Capacitance

1.1 Locate all the components required for this lab and using your breadboard, build the circuit shown in the Lab Preparation section 1. Note we will use a jumper as the switch shown. Measure the resistance of R_1. $R_1 = $ _____ $k\Omega$

1.2 With the power supply off, make sure the capacitor is fully discharged by temporarily touching a jumper across its leads. It will take a fraction of a second to discharge through the jumper then remove it.

1.3 Set the variable power supply (E_{S1}) to 10 VDC and connect your DMM to measure v_c.

1.4 Connect a jumper "switch" to the common (negative rail) position. Calculate the voltage across the capacitor after 1τ ($v_{c@1\tau}$) and set your stopwatch to zero seconds. $v_{c@1\tau} = $ _____ volts

1.5 Turn the power supply on and when you're ready, move the jumper to the "E_{S1}" position and start the stopwatch (or timer) simultaneously. Measure the time it takes for the voltage across the capacitor (v_c) to reach $v_{c@1\tau}$. Record the time it takes to get to 1τ. $\tau = $ _____ seconds

1.6 Use the values you measured for τ and R_1 to determine the value of C_1 in the space provided below. $C_1 = $ _____ μF

1.7 Compare your calculated value for C_1 with what is written on the capacitor body and calculate the percent difference between them in the space provided below. % Diff. = _____ %

1.8 Turn the power supply off and wait at least 30 seconds for the capacitor to discharge.

1.9 Use your DMM to measure the capacitance of C_1. To do this, set your DMM selector switch to the highest capacitance setting (100 μF).

1.10 Make sure the leads are in the correct sockets (between com (black) and capacitance (red)). You will need to look for the socket labeled with the schematic symbol for a capacitor.

1.11 Touch the leads to the capacitor (noting the polarity). Make sure the black lead (common) is in contact with the capacitor lead marked with the black (or "–" strip) and the red lead is in contact with the other capacitor lead.

1.12 Wait for the reading to settle and record the capacitor value. $C_1 = $ _____ μF

1.13 Compare your measured value for C_1 with what is written on the capacitor body and calculate the percent difference between them in the space provided below. % Diff. = _____ %

Note: For full marks, please show *all* your work when performing calculations below:

2. Viewing the Waveforms

2.1 Connect the oscilloscope probe leads from "Channel 1" of the oscilloscope across the capacitor. Please note the polarity of the connection. The alligator clip is the ground (reference) connection while the probe tip is the voltage connection. Ensure the oscilloscope probe has its attenuation set to x1.

2.2 Turn on the oscilloscope and allow it to warm up.

2.3 One the oscilloscope is ready, push the "Default Setup" button and then the "Ch. 1 Menu" button.

2.4 Use the "Volts/Div." knob for channel 1 to set the scale (Y-Axis) to 5 V/Div. The actual value will appear on the bottom of the screen.

2.5 Use the "Sec./Div." knob for channel 1 to set the time base (X-Axis) to 10 s/Div. Again, the actual value will appear on the bottom of the screen.

2.6 With the power supply off, make sure the capacitor is fully discharged by placing a jumper across its leads.

2.7 Connect your jumper "switch" to the ground (negative rail) position, turn the power supply on.

2.8 When the signal trace on the oscilloscope is approximately 1 division away from the left side of the screen, move the jumper on your circuit to the "E_{S1}" position.

2.9 When the signal trace is approximately 1 division away from the right side of the screen, push the "Run/Stop" button.

2.10 Sketch the waveform (with as much detail as possible) on the grids shown below (v_c Charge) and measure v_c after 0τ, 1τ and 5τ?

$v_{c(0\tau)} = $ _____, V $v_{c(1\tau)} = $ _____ V $v_{c(5\tau)} = $ _____ V.

2.11 Push the "Run/Stop" button again and when the signal trace on the oscilloscope is approximately 1 division away from the left side of the screen, move the jumper on your circuit back to the ground (negative rail) position.

2.12 When the signal trace is approximately 1 division away from the right side of the screen, push the "Run/Stop" button.

2.13 Sketch the waveform (with as much detail as possible) on the grids shown below (v_c Discharge) and measure v_c after 0τ, 1τ and 5τ?

$v_{c(0\tau)} = $ _____, V $v_{c(1\tau)} = $ _____ V $v_{c(5\tau)} = $ _____ V.

2.14 Turn off all the equipment.

Louis Jraige

ANALYSIS/OBSERVATIONS:

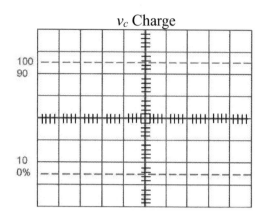

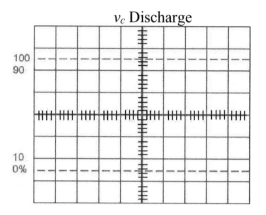

1) Why did the instructor refer to the oscilloscope as a "voltage video camera"?

2) Explain how your calculations compare with your measured data from Section 1 of the procedure?

3) While using an oscilloscope to measure a very small signal, what two dials would you use to "zoom in and out" on the signal?

4) While using an oscilloscope to measure a very small signal, what two dials would you use to "pan" the signal back and forth or up and down?

CONCLUSION:

Please describe in detail which lab objectives you met (if any) and how they were achieved.

After your lab has been signed off and you have cleaned up your work station, please go around to see if others need help and assist (not distract) them. Remember, we assist by making observations and asking questions with our hands behind our backs.

Grade Breakdown Structure

(Refer to your Weekly Lab Rubric or the Sample Rubric posted in your lab manual for more detail.)

	Lab: Capacitors in DC Circuits	Score				
1	Section 1 – Preparation		3	2	1	0
2	Section 2 – Experimentation		3	2	1	0
3	Section 3 – Analysis, Conclusion and Professionalism	4	3	2	1	0
Notes/Comments:		**Total**				
		Teacher's Signature (above)				
		Name				
		Date				

© 2016

Louis Jraige

Inductors in DC Circuits

Name: _____   Course and Section: _____

Partner: _____   Date: _____

PURPOSE:

The purpose of this lab is to become familiar with the following:
1. Verify the basic function of an inductor in an R-L network.
2. Investigate the behaviour of an R-L-C network.
3. To learn to use a function generator to quickly trigger our circuit.
4. Use an oscilloscope to view the voltage developed across an inductor.
5. Use a digital multi-meter (DMM) to measure voltage and inductance.

EQUIPMENT:

1. Your tool and component kits (see your CIS on FOL)
2. Your PPE (untinted/untreated, CSA approved safety glasses with side shields)
3. A breadboard, jumper wires and alligator leads
4. Your DMM (Digital Multi-Meter – MTP 2327)
5. A Dual Trace Oscilloscope, a Variable Voltage DC Power Supply, and a Function Generator
6. Resistors: 100 Ω (1), 330 Ω (1)
7. Inductors: 10 mH (1), 100 mH (1)

PREPARATION: *For full marks, please show **all** your work when performing calculations. Give all answers in engineering notation with prefixes and rounded to three decimals.*

1) Refer to the circuit shown below and determine τ, v_L, and i_L. Also calculate how much time must pass before the network is in steady state. Assume $R_{L1} = 110\ \Omega$

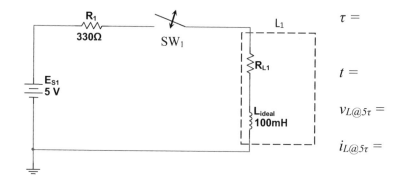

$\tau =$

$t =$

$v_{L@5\tau} =$

$i_{L@5\tau} =$

Please Note: *Be sure to have read the documents labeled "The Basics of Creating and Using Graphs" (Appendix F), "Inductors and their Code Schemes" (Appendix H), "The Oscilloscope" (Appendix I) and "The Function Generator" (Appendix J) prior to completing the pre-lab.*

2) *Refer to the circuit shown above and calculate v_{L1} at 0τ, 1τ and 5τ for both the store and release cycles. Then, plot both the store and release cycles against both time and τ. Please use the scaling of 222 microseconds per division. Note that the store cycle starts at $t = 0s$ and the release cycle starts at $t = 1.554$ ms.*

     Please Note: *In addition to the items listed in the rubric, this pre-lab will be worth all 3 of the lab "preparation" marks; 1 mark for each of the Sections (1, 2 and 3) of the Pre-Lab. Remember to use the correct algebraic manipulation of the equations (with variables and subscripts) then number substitution and final answer in standard engineering notation (with prefixes) and the proper units. When sketching the wiring diagram, please use the appropriate standards and conventions shown.*

Store Cycle Calculations:

Release Cycle Calculations:

Louis Jraige

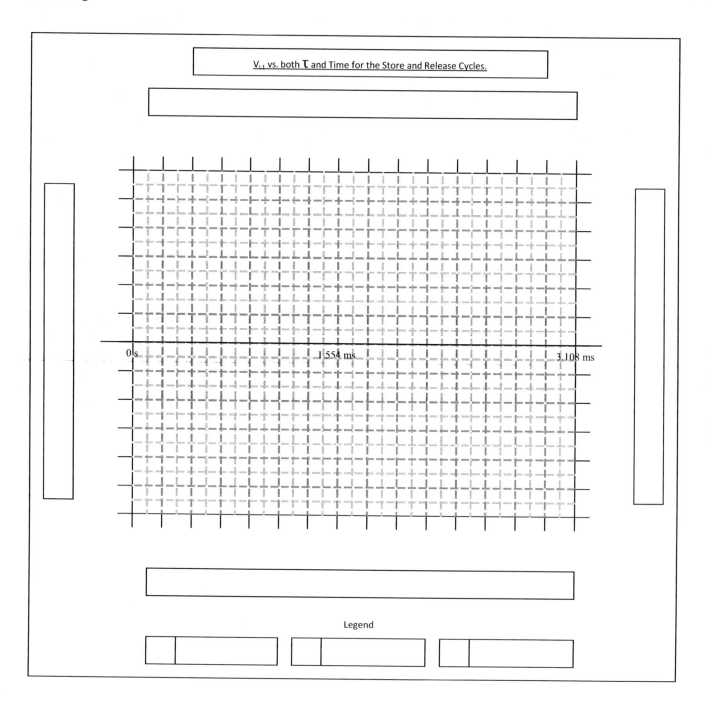

V_{i_1} vs. both τ and Time for the Store and Release Cycles.

0 s   1.554 ms   3.108 ms

Legend

3) *Refer to the circuit shown above and calculate i_{L1} at 0τ, 1τ and 5τ for both the store and release cycles. Then, plot both the store and release cycles against both time and τ. Please use the scaling of 222 microseconds per division. Note that the store cycle starts at $t = 0s$ and the release cycle starts at $t = 1.554$ ms.*

      Please Note: *In addition to the items listed in the rubric, this pre-lab will be worth all 3 of the lab "preparation" marks; 1 mark for each of the Sections (1, 2 and 3) of the Pre-Lab. Remember to use the correct algebraic manipulation of the equations (with variables and subscripts) then number substitution and final answer in standard engineering notation (with prefixes) and the proper units. When sketching the wiring diagram, please use the appropriate standards and conventions shown.*

Store Cycle Calculations:

Release Cycle Calculations:

Louis Jraige

i$_{L1}$ vs. both τ and Time for the Store and Release Cycles.

0 s   1.554 ms   3.108 ms

Legend

© 2016   108

DESIGN INTENT:

In this lab, we will learn how to use an oscilloscope to "view" inductor characteristics. We will electrically "tap" on the inductor and observe the voltage "ring". Be sure to have read the documents labeled "The Basics of Creating and Using Graphs" (Appendix F), "Inductors and their Code Schemes" (Appendix H), "The Oscilloscope" (Appendix I) and "The Function Generator" (Appendix J) prior to completing the lab.

BACKGROUND DATA:

TEXTBOOK REFERENCE:

Louis Jraige

PROCEDURE:

1. **Using the Function Generator and Oscilloscope**
   1.1 Turn on both the function generator and the oscilloscope and allow them to start up.
   1.2 Set the channel 1 of the oscilloscope to 2.00 Volts/Div. with DC coupling and a time base of 2.5 ms.
   1.3 Set the oscilloscope to "Edge" trigger on the "Rising" slope and adjust the level to 1 subdivision above the (center) zero line.
   1.4 Connect the output of the function generator to the channel 1 (CH 1) input of the oscilloscope.
   1.5 Set the function generator to produce a square wave output at 100 Hz. (⌐⌐_⌐)
   1.6 Set the amplitude (magnitude) of the signal to 5 V with a 2.5 V DC offset so that the signal toggles from 0VDC to 5 VDC.
   1.7 Sketch the waveform (with as much detail as possible) on the grid shown below.

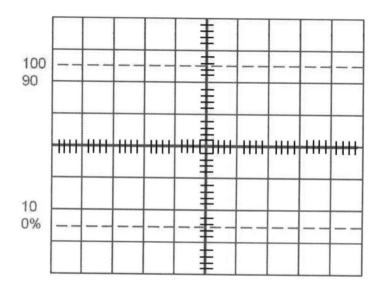

   1.8 Shut off the function generator.

2. Viewing the Inductor Waveforms (R-L Network)

2.1 Locate all the components required for this lab and using your DMM, measure the following values.

$R_1 =$ _____ Ω, $L_1 =$ _____ mH and $R_{L1} =$ _____ Ω

2.2 Using your breadboard, build the circuit shown below.

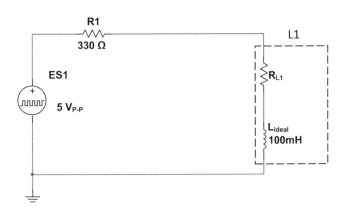

2.3 Without changing any of the parameters, connect the function generator to the circuit.

2.4 Again, without changing any of the parameters, connect the oscilloscope's channel 1 input across the inductor.

2.5 Sketch the waveform (with as much detail as possible) on the grid shown below.

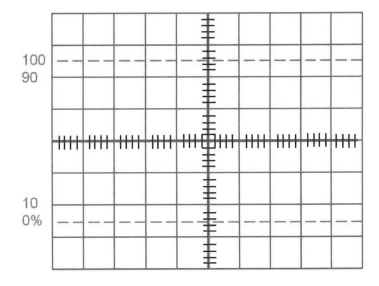

2.6 Shut off the function generator.

3. Measuring the Inductance of an Inductor   *(Optional In-Class Demonstration)*

3.1 Turn on both the function generator and the oscilloscope and allow them to start up.

3.2 Locate the 100 Ω resistor and the 10 mH inductor. Using a DMM, measure the following values.

$R_1 =$ _____ Ω, and $L_1 =$ _____ mH and $R_{L1} =$ _____ Ω

3.3 Build the circuit shown below but swap the position of the resistor and inductor.

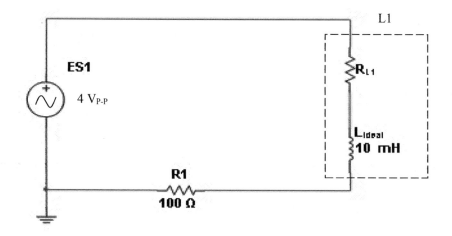

3.4 Connect the oscilloscope to the circuit such that channel 1 measures E_{S1} and channel 2 measures V_{R1}. Move the channel 1 trace to 2 divisions above the center line and the channel 2 trace to 2 divisions below the center line

3.5 Reset the oscilloscope. Now, set the oscilloscope's time base to 100 μs/DIV, channel 1 to 2 V/DIV and channel 2 to 1 V/DIV.

3.6 Set the function generator to produce a 4 V_{P-P} sinusoidal waveform at 60 Hz.

3.7 Now, set the function generator to the 10 kHz range with a range factor of 0 (zero).

3.8 "Sweep" through all the frequencies between 0 Hz. and 10 kHz. Try to set the function generator to the frequency that produces a resistor voltage of 2 V_{P-P}. Please note that as you adjust the frequency, you may have to "tweek" E_{S1} so that it stays at exactly 4 V/DIV.

3.9 Once you have located the frequency where $V_{R1} = E_{S1} / 2$, determine L_1 below.
Remember, $L_1 = (\sqrt{3} * R_1) / (2\pi * f)$.

$f =$ _____ kHz., and $L_1 =$ _____

ANALYSIS/OBSERVATIONS:

1) What role did R_{L1} play in the circuit?

2) Why did we have to include R_{L1} in all calculations?

3) What do you think would happen to the "ringing" (Section 3) waveform if R_{L1} was increased and/or decreased?

4) Make an observation on the store and release phase curves; explain why they look the way they do? Be sure to consider cycle direction, amplitude and other attributes in your description.

Louis Jraige

CONCLUSION:

Please describe in detail which lab objectives you met (if any) and how they were achieved.

After your lab has been signed off and you have cleaned up your work station, please go around to see if others need help and assist (not distract) them. Remember, we assist by making observations and asking questions with our hands behind our backs.

Grade Breakdown Structure

(Refer to your Weekly Lab Rubric or the Sample Rubric posted in your lab manual for more detail.)

	Lab: Inductors in DC Circuits	Score				
1	Section 1 – Preparation		3	2	1	0
2	Section 2 – Experimentation		3	2	1	0
3	Section 3 – Analysis, Conclusion and Professionalism	4	3	2	1	0
Notes/Comments:		Total				
		Teacher's Signature (above)				
		Name				
		Date				

Louis Jraige

Made in the USA
Columbia, SC
21 July 2023

20696119R00074